Basic Skills in

NEAB GCSE English

Imelda Pilgrim

Consultants: Peter Buckroyd
Chief Examiner for NEAB English

John Nield
Principal Examiner for NEAB English

Heinemann

NEAB/AQA

Heinemann Educational Publishers
Halley Court, Jordan Hill, Oxford OX2 8EJ
A division of Reed Educational and Professional Publishing Ltd

OXFORD MELBOURNE AUCKLAND
JOHANNESBURG BLANTYRE GABORONE
IBADAN PORTSMOUTH (NH) USA CHICAGO

First published 1998

02 01 00 99
10 9 8 7 6 5 4 3

ISBN 0 435 10409 8

Designed and produced by Gecko Ltd, Bicester, Oxon
Cover illustration by Arlene Adams
Printed and bound in Spain by Edelvives

Acknowledgements
The Authors and Publishers would like to thank the following for permission to use photographs/copyright material.

Beehive Communications for the cover of a Eurolines leaflet, p5; *The Northern Echo* for the articles 'Nightmare fate of a dream machine' by Nigel Burton 'Stray dogs on increase' (31 and 27 Dec. 1997), pp11, 49; D.C. Thomson & Co for 'Magical day' in *The Sunday Post* (Dec. 21, 1997), the Sagittarius Horoscope and the articles 'Gambling' and 'Why do you bully me?' featured in *Shout* magazine (Editions 118 and 127), pp13, 19, 93, 124–5; Association of Teachers and Lecturers for extracts from 'Crime and Punishment' (ATL, *Report*, June/July, 1997), p14–5; Halifax plc for article, 'You are in the driving seat of tomorrow's world' (Summer, 1997) and extract, 'Get a life, don't be a boozer loser' (Spring, 1997) from *Quest* magazine (Summer, 1997), pp17, 87; Virgin Megastores for an advertisement 'Get ready for a summer of festivals' (1997), p18; Mencap for extract from Blue Sky Appeal Bulletin, January 1997, p19; South Lakes Wild Animal Park for extracts from leaflet, pp20–1; Save the Children Fund for extract from leaflet 'Urgent Stop Press!' and logo and slogan, pp23, 24; *The Guardian* for charts 'Then and Now – where our money goes' (Aug. 30, 1997), p23; Wensleydale Creamery for extracts from leaflet, p24–5; Anrdman Animations Ltd for the 'Wallace & Gromit' image, p24; Solo Syndication Ltd on behalf of *You* magazine for caption 'Are Men afraid of Women's magazines', 'Do Children Get a Fair Share of Dad?' (Jan. 18, 1998), on behalf of *The Mail on Sunday* for an extract from the article 'Homes fit for the future' (Dec. 28, 1997) pp26, 84; *Sugar* Magazine for caption of article 'Wrecking their own lives' (Jan. 98), an extract from the article '15 things you just got to do this year' (Feb. 98), pp26, 76; The Christian Children's Fund of Great Britain for extract from Appeal advertisement, p27; World Society for Protection of Animals for extracts from advertisement 'Setting free the Bears', p28; Butlin's Ltd for extracts from holiday brochure, p30; Club 18-30 for extract from holiday brochure, p31; Hambleton District Council for extracts from the Thirsk Swimming Pool Autumn-Winter programme, p32; Center Parcs for extract from holiday brochure, p33; *Men's Health* magazine for extract from article 'Kickboxing/M'ua Thai' (Feb. 98), extract 'Eat fat, stay slim', pp34, 38; *Health and Fitness* magazine for extract from article 'Karate', the question and answer in 'Solutions' (Feb. 98), pp34, 38; *The Times Educational Supplement* for extract 'PE curb danger to UK Health' (Jan. 23, 1998) extract from article 'Messing about on early manoeuvres' by Phil Revell, (Feb. 98) the headline 'Work in shops till the grades drop' (Feb. 6, 1998), pp35, 90, 112; Oxford University Press for extract 'What is health?' from *P.E. to 16* (1996), the poem 'Limbo' from *The Arrivants* by Edward Kamau Brathwaite, pp37, 54; *Bliss* Magazine for extract 'Work it, girl' (Mar. 98), p38; Random House UK Ltd on behalf of the Estate of Robert Frost for the poem 'The Road Not Taken' from *The Poetry of Robert Frost* edited by Edward Connery Lathem, published by Jonathan Cape Ltd, the poem 'Unrelated Incidents' from *Intimate Voices: Selected Works 1965–1983* by Tom Leonard, published by Vintage, extract from *An Evil Cradling* by Brian Keenan (Hutchinson), extract from *Of Mice and Men* by John Steinbeck (William Heinemann), pp40, 61, 100, 103–4; James Berry for his poem 'Song of the Sea and People', p45; Reed Educational and Professional Publishing, Australia, for the poem 'But you Didn't' by Merrill Glass, p.47, Spike Milligan Production Ltd for the poem 'Dog Lovers' by Spike Milligan, p48; Faber and Faber Ltd for the poem 'The Bat' by Theodore Roethke from *Collected Poems*, p51; The Peters Fraser and Dunlop Group Ltd on behalf of Roger McGough for the poem 'Nooligan' from *In the Classroom*, published by Jonathan Cape Ltd, p55; Marian Reiner on behalf of Judith Thurman for the poem 'Clockface' from *Flashlight and Other Poems* by Judith Thurman © 1976 Judith Thurman, p56; 'Change' on p57. Copyright © 1970, renewed 1998 by Charlotte Zolotow. Reprinted by permission of S©ott Treimel New York; Little Brown & Company (UK) for the poem 'Island man' from *The Fat Black Woman's Poems* by Grace Nichols, published by Virago Press and for an extract from *I Know Why the Caged Bird Sings* by Maya Angelou (Virago Press), pp62, 105; Penguin UK for the poem 'Attention Seeking' by Jackie Kay from *Three Has Gone* published by Blackie, p64; Vernon Scannell for his poem 'Incendiary', p63; Wella Great Britain for the text on a hair product sachet, p72–3; Egmont Children's Books Ltd for a recipe 'Banana Frothies' from *The Teddy Bear Cookbook*, published by Octopus Books Ltd, p72; The Controller of Her Majesty's Stationery Office for an extract from Crown copyright leaflets 'Don't Lose Your Vote' and 'Guide to Hours of Employment and Prohibited Employment', pp74, 111; Health Education Authority for extracts from leaflets 'A Parents Guide to Drugs and Alcohol' and 'D-Mag', p75; Shelter for their Appeal letter 'Will the next person you see sleeping rough still be alive in the morning?' and an extract from Crisis Winterwatch Survey 1995-6, pp78, 82; *The Big Issue* for an extract from article 'Problems of Alcohol' by Delia O'Hennessy (Jun. 30, 1995) sourced from *Essential Articles IV*, the resource for file for issues, Carel Press, p86; Rough Guides Ltd for extract from 'Between Two Cultures' by Smita Patel in *More Women Travel: A Rough Guides Special* (3rd Edition) by Miranda Davies and Natania Jansz. © 1995, p92; the article 'Danger! Children at work' sourced from *Essential Articles IV*, the resource file for issues, Carel Press, p110.

The Publishers have made every effort to trace the copyright holders, but if they have inadvertently overlooked any, they will be pleased to make the necessary arrangements at the first opportunity.

The Publishers would like to thank the following for permission to reproduce photographs on the pages noted.

Car Magazine/Tim Wren, p11; Direct Holidays, p31; Oxford Scientific Films/Stephen Dalton, p51; Sally & Richard Greenhill, p78; Roger Scruton, p82; Iain Dalzel-Job, p90; Bubbles/Ian West, p112; Bubbles/David Robinson, p122.

Contents

Section A
READING

Section B
WRITING

Section C
EXAM PRACTICE

How to use this book

To prepare for your GCSE in English you will need to develop your skills in reading and writing. This book takes you through the skills you will need to focus on, building on what you already know and showing you how to develop further.

Although reading and writing are dealt with separately in this book – to make it easier to follow – in reality they are very closely linked and often overlap. You will find that the work you do on reading helps you with your writing and vice versa. You can choose to work through the sections in the order they appear in the book or to alternate between 'Reading' and 'Writing'.

As you work through the book you will:

- learn more about the specific skills you need in the examinations
- find a wide range of texts and activities designed to help you develop these skills
- work through examples of the kinds of question that are set in the examinations
- learn how to read the questions carefully
- learn how to plan and write your answers.

There are also practice papers for you to try, with advice on how to do them, and specimen papers for you to work through on your own when you are ready.

As you study the texts and work through the activities, you will become more aware of what you are expected to do in the examinations. You will gain in confidence and your skills in English will steadily improve. The effort you make now will help you to prepare for GCSE English and achieve your best in the examinations.

Your skills in English

Just think of how many things you are asked to read or write in a single school day.

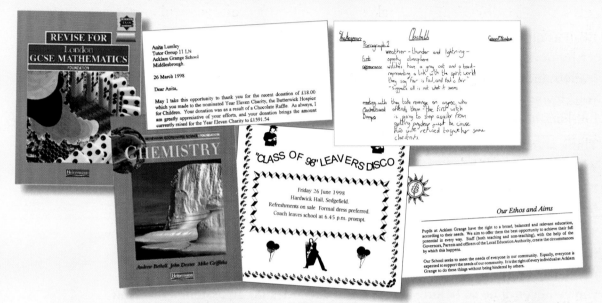

Your reading and writing skills affect how well you do in almost every area of your school life. They will continue to be important to you throughout your life, whether or not you continue with full-time education.

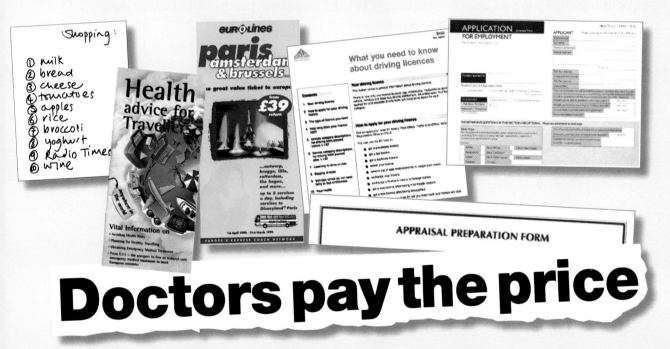

There are many ways, apart from using this book, by which you can improve your reading and writing.

Developing your reading and writing skills

Read as often as you can and as many different things as you can. Make a point of trying to read a newspaper once or twice a week. Look around you and read the leaflets and adverts that are often on display in public places. Find out more about your favourite sport or interest by reading a magazine about it. If you don't like full-length stories opt for short ones that can be read in half an hour.

Think about the things you are reading. Ask yourself whether they work well – whether they achieve what they set out to do. When you come across new words, use a dictionary to find out what they mean and start to use them in your own writing.

Think about the way you write and the way other people write. Look at the ways ideas are organized and sentences put together. Start to experiment with new methods and set yourself targets: organize your notes with sub-headings if you've never done so before; aim to write two sides for an assignment if you usually write one.

By becoming more aware of the reading material that surrounds you in your daily life, and by transferring what you learn through reading into your own writing, you will make steady progress in both areas. What's more, the progress you make now will stand you in good stead all your life.

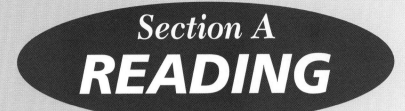

Section A
READING

Reading Non-Fiction Texts

Non-fiction texts are those that are *not* made up. They are based on real life, personal experience, facts and/or opinions. They include autobiographies, biographies, journals, diaries, travel writing, leaflets, newspaper articles, factual and informative materials.

In this section you will learn how to:

- read for meaning
- think about presentation
- look at language
- choose the right material.

Reading of non-fiction texts is tested in NEAB GCSE English, Paper 1 Section A.

Reading for meaning

Fact and opinion

The following statements are *facts*.

- A layer of air called the atmosphere surrounds the earth.
- More than 70% of the earth's surface is covered by oceans and seas.
- The earth is one of nine planets that move around the sun.

They can be checked and proved.

The following statements are *opinions*.

- The earth is a beautiful place.
- There is probably life on other planets.
- Too much money is spent on space exploration.

They cannot be proved. They are simply statements of a point of view.

A *fact* is something that can be proved to be true whereas an *opinion* cannot.

ACTIVITY 1

Draw a table with two columns, one headed **fact** and one headed **opinion**, like the example below.

FACT	OPINION

Sort the following statements about cars into **facts** and **opinions**.

- Car pollution will probably destroy our planet.
- A car usually has four or five different gears.
- Most cars have petrol or diesel engines.
- The car is man's best friend.
- Cars were invented in the nineteenth century.
- People shouldn't have more than one car.
- The maximum speed allowed in England is 70 mph.
- It is difficult to pass your driving test.

Separating fact from opinion

Many things you read are a mixture of *fact* and *opinion*. You need to be able to separate them. To do this you need to read very carefully. Sometimes you have to break the sentences down and then rewrite the ideas in your own words. You can't just copy them out.

Read the following newspaper article. It is a mixture of *facts* and *opinions*.

Nightmare fate of a dream machine

By NIGEL BURTON

IT was a Christmas present dreams are made of – a Ferrari F355 Spider resplendent in Italian racing red paintwork, sitting on beautiful alloy wheels.

The driver's wife had bought the hand-made dream machine for £103,000 as the ultimate gift for her car crazy husband.

The thrilled new owner couldn't wait to take it out for a spin.

But a short while later the driver's face was as red as the Ferrari's paintwork – and his car was only fit for a very long stay in the garage bodyshop.

Cleveland Police said the driver lost control along a stretch of road in Thornaby and his dream machine slammed into a metal barrier nose first. The impact spun the car round and shunted its rear

■ **Classic car: A gleaming Ferrari in Italian racing red**

into the guard rail. Luckily, the new owner – who had done just 124 miles before the calamitous accident – walked away from the wreck shocked but unscathed.

Police generously declined to name the car's owner last night to spare him from further embarrassment.

'As if it wasn't bad enough smashing up such an expensive car, to wreck the wife's Christmas present must have added insult to injury,' said a force spokesman.

The car was removed by recovery men and taken to a specialist repairer on Tyneside for repairs which could cost as much as £30,000.

Garageman Graham Abel, who recovered the damaged car, said: 'At least he must have plenty of money to get it fixed. It isn't every Christmas you find a Ferrari in your Christmas stocking.'

NORTHERN ECHO

ACTIVITY 2

Reread the first paragraph. The **facts** in it are that:

● the car was a Ferrari F355 Spider

● the colour of the paintwork was Italian racing red

● it had alloy wheels.

The **opinions** are that:

● it was a Christmas present dreams are made of

● the wheels were beautiful.

Write down four more **facts** and four more **opinions** taken from the rest of the article. There may be times when you are not sure whether a phrase is a fact or an opinion. Only write down the ones you are certain of.

Checking the facts

1 Surveys

A *survey* is a general look at or examination of a particular issue. It is usually carried out through the use of a questionnaire in which people are asked to give answers to different questions. Their answers are then collected together to produce statistics. As a result of a survey something may appear to be a 'fact'. It may, however, be based on very little real evidence.

Think about this survey result:

> 40% of school leavers have no plans for the future.

What if the school leavers were all from the same school where careers advice was poor? This might explain why so many of them had no plans for the future. It wouldn't necessarily be true of 40% of *all* school leavers.

ACTIVITY 3

Think about these survey results and then answer the questions that follow them.

> School children spend 60% of their money on sweets.

What difference might the age of the children questioned make to the results of the survey?

> Eight out of ten people are going to take a holiday abroad this year.

What difference would it make if the survey was done outside a travel agent's?

Always think carefully about how surveys may have been carried out before accepting the results as facts.

2 Editorials

Most newspapers have an *editorial* or *leader* linked to an item that is in the news. In these articles the editor is generally expressing his or her own opinion and wants to influence the way the reader thinks.

Read the editorial on page 13 in which the editor develops the personal viewpoint that all the effort made in the run-up to Christmas is worth it in the end.

Magical day

IT'S BEEN an intense year, what with one thing and another. And it's been anything but relaxing these past few weeks.

Christmas shopping seems to get more and more frenetic, and every year we vow we'll never do it again.

But come Thursday morning the stress will be forgotten as excited children tear at brightly-coloured paper and squeal with delight as they find Santa has come up trumps again.

It's then that even the most exhausted and jaundiced parents will find themselves suddenly filled with the elusive Christmas spirit.

And later on, when the kids are tucked up in bed and the family have all gone home, they'll be able to reflect that it was all worthwhile.

In a dark and troubled world, it's worth a bit of effort to light up your own small corner for one magical day.

Merry Christmas, everyone.

SUNDAY POST

ACTIVITY 4

Look at the number of times the editor writes **opinions** as though they were facts:

- It's been an intense year
- every year we vow we'll never do it again
- come Thursday morning the stress will be forgotten.

How many other examples can you find? Write them down.

Notice that there are **no facts** in this editorial.

ACTIVITY 5

Write an **editorial** of your own which develops the point of view that Christmas is *not* worth all the effort people put into it. Here are some opinions to help you:

- it's too expensive
- people end up in debt
- children want too much
- families argue at Christmas time
- people eat and drink too much
- too many people are on their own at Christmas
- things are much cheaper in the sales.

Following an argument

When a writer makes a case for something or against something, s/he is presenting the reader with an argument. So, for example, a writer may develop an argument in favour of lowering the school-leaving age. Another may argue that schooling should be compulsory to the age of eighteen. Yet another may argue that it should be for the pupils' parents to decide when their child should leave school.

In order to build an argument the writer must develop his/her point of view.

In order to follow an argument you need to be able to:

● spot the key points that the writer is making

● write these in your own words.

Read this article about the effects on children when a parent is put in prison. Then work through Activity 6.

Children of prisoners suffer in a similar way to those whose parents divorce or even die. The loss of the parent is just as sudden, unexpected and upsetting.

Family income may drop sharply and there may be other practical difficulties. The remaining parent could become depressed, feel isolated and be worried about being able to cope.

A good relationship between the child and the imprisoned parent often depends on what the child is told and yet many parents find it difficult to give an honest and straightforward explanation of what is happening. In an effort to protect their children, they may not tell them the truth. The story they are told can, however, be even more upsetting than the truth. For instance, a child who is told that the imprisoned parent is in hospital, might know of someone who has died in hospital and may fear that this is what has happened to the missing mother or father.

There are many other excuses that families use to explain the absence of the parent. But the children themselves will know that something is not quite right. Children have the ability to accept and deal with difficult situations. It is important to listen to them and to tell them what they need to know.

REPORT

ACTIVITY 6

The writer clearly states what the argument is in the first paragraph. It is that 'children of prisoners suffer' from the loss of the parent. Several points are made to support this point of view.

The sentences below contain the **key points** of each paragraph. Read each paragraph again, then write out the sentences, filling in the space with the correct word from the list below.

- Children of prisoners have the same problems as those whose parents _____ or _____ .

- The family _____ may drop and the remaining parent may become _____ .

- It is important to tell the child the _____ yet many parents do not do this and the child becomes even more _____ .

- Children should be given the chance to _____ with difficult situations and it is important to _____ to them.

> depressed   die   listen   truth   income   upset   divorce   deal

Now read the advice that is given to teachers on how to help children of prisoners:

Advice to teachers

It is vital that teachers recognize the difficulties facing prisoners' families. They can help the children in many ways.

- Teachers must let both parents and pupils know that they can be approached if the need should arise. This offer must be made to *all* children – many families do not give information for fear of being rejected, so teachers may be unaware that the parent is in prison.

- Any name-calling or bullying must be dealt with. Children need to be able to tell a teacher when this happens. They also need someone on whom they can offload their feelings of loss and separation, someone who will listen without judging them.

- The offer of practical help is always useful. Guidance on free school meals or uniforms can lessen the financial pressure on some families – and consequently make life easier for the children.

REPORT

ACTIVITY 7

It is important not to simply accept everything a writer says as being correct. You need to think carefully about the points that are made and decide:
- whether you agree or disagree with them
- whether there are different points to be considered.

Here are some questions for you to think about:
- Do all children whose parents go to prison suffer?
- Are there any circumstances where it might be better not to tell the child the truth?
- Is the age of the child important? What difference does this make?
- Why do so many parents find it difficult to give their children 'an honest and straightforward answer'?
- Can all children 'accept and deal with difficult situations'?

You may finally decide you agree with the writer but it is important to always question the assumptions that are made in an article such as this.

ACTIVITY 8

1   Pick out and write down the key points in the advice to teachers. Remember to put them in your own words.

2   Reread both parts of the article and the key points you have written again. Is there anything important that you think has been missed out? If there is add it to your key points.

3   Using your key points, answer the following question.

    What does the writer tell us about the children of prisoners?

Test *yourself*

1   What is a fact?

    What is an opinion?

2   Write down:

    - five facts about your school

    - five opinions about your school.

3   Read the text opposite carefully.

    What is the argument about?

4   List two facts and two opinions from the article.

5   List the key points of the article. Remember to write them down in your own words.

6   Using your list of key points to help you, explain how the writer thinks we can save fossil fuels. Make sure you only use the key points to answer the question.

ECO-ISSUES

YOU ARE IN THE DRIVING SEAT OF TOMORROW'S WORLD!

Let's face it, the kids of today are the adults of tomorrow – so what you do today will affect the world you and your friends will live in as grown-ups.

We've all got to do what we can to save our planet by saving its natural resources. Fossil fuels like coal, gas and oil are three of our most precious 'buried treasures'. It is fossil fuels that create the energy which is used to heat our homes and to run our power stations. They are also used to make petrol and diesel for our cars.

As more and more cars are produced, our roads are becoming more and more congested and the atmosphere is becoming more polluted by the poisonous fumes emitted from exhaust pipes.

If we used our cars less, we would need less fossil fuels and would cause less pollution in the atmosphere.

Talk to Mum and Dad and see if your family could use the car less. Are there times when you could leave the car at home and take a bus or train instead?

Why not encourage Mum or Dad to cycle to work occasionally? It's often quicker, needs no fuel, causes no pollution and it would keep them fit!

If that's not possible, perhaps they could share the journey with a neighbour or workmate? How many cars do you see with just one person in them? Loads! What a waste!

When replacing your car ask your parents to buy one which is more energy efficient – many models can now do 60 or even 70 miles per gallon. They'll save money and help to save fossil fuels.

Remember, with just a little extra effort we can all help to make tomorrow's world a better place.

Thinking about presentation

Types of text

There are many different *kinds* of writing, such as:

- letters
- adverts
- notes
- stories
- horoscopes
- news-sheets.

Letters

> Dear Sir,
>
> I am a fifteen-year-old boy who is very interested in following a career in the sport and leisure industry. My school offers all its Year 10 pupils the opportunity to do two weeks' work experience in June and I was wondering if it would be possible to gain a placement with your company . . .

Adverts

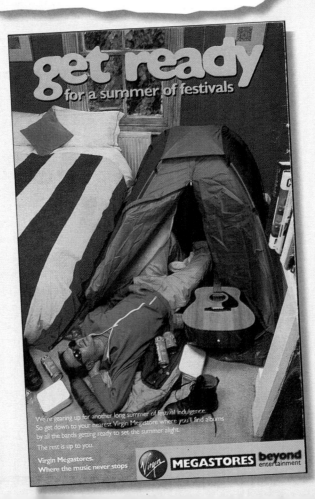

Notes

VOLCANOES:

- ◆ approx. 850 active volcanoes in the world
- ◆ caused by movement of rock in the earth's surface
- ◆ most are found in the Ring of Fire around the Pacific Ocean
- ◆ can erupt with little warning
- ◆ release red hot ash and lava
- ◆ between eruptions they are called dormant.

Stories

It was a cold, dark night in the middle of winter when he first heard the voice. It came creeping into his dreams, waking him gently but turning his blood cold as he realized he was no longer sleeping. Softly, hauntingly, it called to him, forcing him to leave his bed and move hesitantly across the room towards the shimmering frost-cracked window.

Horoscopes

SAGITTARIUS
November 23–December 22

LADS: Although your mate's lad is big trouble, try not to interfere cos they need to sort it out for themselves.
LOOKS: Your make-up doesn't have to be expensive — bargain buys work just as well.
LAUGHS: Things might not go exactly as planned this fortnight but that doesn't mean you won't have a fab time anyway!
LUCK: Try not to jump to conclusions if you want to stay popular.

LUCKY DAY: TUESDAY 2

SHOUT MAGAZINE

News-sheets

The City backs Mencap

ON December 5th 1996, leading derivatives broker Intercapital donated half their revenue and commissions to Mencap as part of the annual Intercapital Charity Day.

This raised approximately £160,000 for the Appeal.

Brokers at Intercapital had the choice of either staying in bed, or going in to trade and make money for charity.

They turned up in force, some in fancy dress and armed with champagne, to make the day one to remember.

BLUE SKY APPEAL BULLETIN

Can you think of any other types of writing? Make a list of them.

We use the word *text* to talk about these different kinds of written material.

How information is presented

Some of the texts you read use particular features to present the ideas. These features are known as *presentational devices*.

The first step in being able to write about presentational devices is to identify them.

Look at the leaflet, which has part of its cover on this page and some of its contents on the next page, advertising an animal park.

ACTIVITY 1

The labels around the leaflet are numbered.

1 Make a list of the numbers in your exercise book.

2 Choose the description from the box below which you think matches the label. Write it beside the correct number.

heading	sub-headings
photographs	map
bold print	direct question
use of colour	different print size
timetable	logo
slogan	

3 **4** **5** **6**

Safari Railway • Children's Farm • Lake View Café • Gift Shop • Picnic Areas

South Lakes *Wild* Animal Park

The Lake District's only zoological park is recognized as one of Europe's leading conservation zoos.

The rolling 17 acres are home to the rarest animals on earth. They are participants in co-ordinated breeding programmes to save them from almost certain extinction in the wild.

We are the only zoo in Britain to hold both Amur and Sumatran Tigers, the biggest and smallest tigers left in the world.

We have been called the most animal friendly zoo in Britain because of our unique way of looking after the animals. Many animals have complete freedom to wander at will, such as lemurs, kangaroos, wallabies and exotic deer. Parrots fly freely in the trees. So if you want a great day out and wish to help the vital work of conserving the natural world, then there is only one place you can do it, South Lakes Wild Animal Park.

new for 97

Red Panda
White Rhinoceros
Maned Wolves
Cheetah
Otters

daily events

12.00pm Meet a snake and cure any fears.

1.00pm Meet the Owls display and talk.

2.00pm Lemur feeding. You can help the keepers.

2.30pm Tiger feeding. Unique in Europe!!!

3.00pm All the many other animals get fed.

Why not leave the car behind and take the Zoo bus?

The Stagecoach Service X18 from Bowness-on-Windermere brings you via Newby Bridge and Ulverston directly to the park then returns later in the day.

(Whitsun Holiday and Summer only).

Enjoy your day, your visit will help our vital work.

admission

Adults	£3.75
Child (3-16)	£2.75
O.A.Ps	£2.75
Family of 2 adults, 2 children	£10.25

How to find us

Eskdale
Ravenglass
Broughton-in-Furness
Coniston
Ambleside
Windermere
Kendal
A590
DALTON-IN-FURNESS
Barrow-in-Furness
M6

opening times

1st April to 30th September 10am-6pm
1st October to 31st March 10am-Dusk
Closed: 25th December

South Lakes Wild Animal Park, Crossgates, Dalton-in-Furness, Cumbria LA15 8JR   Telephone: 01229 466086

7 **8** **9** **10** **11**

ACTIVITY 2

Once you have identified the main **presentational devices** in a text you can then write about them. Read through the following instructions for advice on how to do this task.

Write about the **presentational devices** used in this leaflet and say what is important about them.

1   Your first step is to make notes. Look again at the leaflet on the South Lakes Animal Park and write a sentence or more about each of the following:

● the way colour is used

● the different sizes and kinds of print

● the appeal of the photographs

● the reason the map is there

● the importance of the logo and the slogan

● anything else you think is important about the presentation of the leaflet.

2   Now that you have made your notes you can start putting together your answer.

Here is an example of how you could do this:

Bright colours are used in the leaflet to make it more attractive and to help separate out the different bits of information. The name of the place is printed in large print at the top and the word Wild looks as though it's handwritten. This might make the reader feel that unusual and strange things might happen here. The sub-headings are all written in yellow print so that particular pieces of information will stand out clearly. Other information is written in white print on a coloured background or in ordinary type. The information about the tigers and the question about the car are written in bold print so that they stand out more clearly. The leaflet includes photographs of animals and a map. The photographs show you what you will see and the map tells you how to get there. There is also a logo and slogan on the leaflet. They both emphasize the importance of conservation and make the reader think about this.

3   Add to the sample answer above any other points you think are important.

More about presentation

Other *presentational devices* you may come across include italics and underlining and graphs and diagrams.

Italics and <u>underlining</u>

These are used when a writer wants to emphasize something. For example:

The giant panda has become a symbol of conservation across the world. This is partly because there are *only a few hundred* giant pandas still surviving in the wild.

URGENT STOP PRESS!!

Every penny counts.

The Royal Mint estimates that there are 7 billion pennies in the UK. Yet at least one third of them are sitting idle in old jam jars, milk bottles and down the backs of sofas.

<u>That means 20 million pounds worth of cash is literally doing nothing!</u>

Graphs and diagrams

These are used when a writer wants to show you information in a different, more visual way. What information are you given in the following diagram?

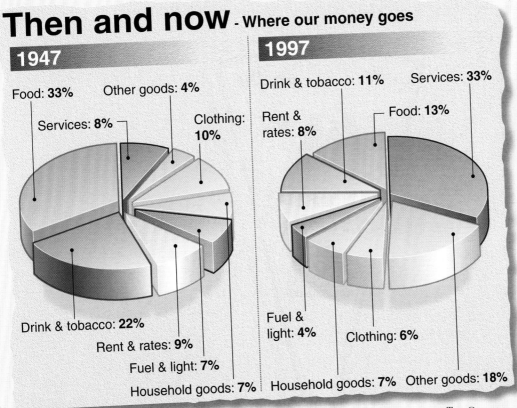

Then and now - Where our money goes

1947

Food: **33%**
Other goods: **4%**
Services: **8%**
Clothing: **10%**
Drink & tobacco: **22%**
Rent & rates: **9%**
Fuel & light: **7%**
Household goods: **7%**

1997

Drink & tobacco: **11%**
Services: **33%**
Rent & rates: **8%**
Food: **13%**
Fuel & light: **4%**
Clothing: **6%**
Household goods: **7%**
Other goods: **18%**

THE GUARDIAN

Test *yourself*

1   What is a text?

2   Name each of the presentational devices used in the following extracts:

a   Please help us <u>make every penny count</u>. Empty those jam jars, look under the sofa cushions and unearth those forgotten pennies.

b   **Then and now** – where our money goes

c   The rolling 17 acres are home to the rarest animals on earth.

We are the only zoo in Britain to hold both Amur and Sumatran Tigers, the biggest and smallest tigers left in the world.

We have been called the most animal friendly zoo in Britain.

d   The giant panda is a large black and white creature which feeds on bamboo shoots. They are very rare and, if nothing is done, could become *extinct* in the wild.

e

3   Read the following text carefully. Pay attention to the presentational devices.

Opening Times

Mon - Sat 9.30am to 5.00pm
Sunday 10.00am to 4.30pm
Please note that the optimum time for
viewing cheesemaking is
between 10.30am and 3.00pm.
The 'Cheese Experience' tour takes
30-90 minutes.

ADMISSION

Adult £2.00 Child £1.50
Schools £1.50
Family Ticket £6.50
Guided Tours £2.50
Coach party booking
essential.

PARKING

There is ample free
parking on site.
Coaches can be
accommodated
by appointment.

Wensleydale Dairy Products
Wensleydale Creamery
Gayle Lane
Hawes
North Yorkshire DL8 3RN
Telephone: 01969 667664
Fax: 01969 667638
E-mail:
creamery@wensleydale.co.uk
Website:
http://www.wensleydale.co.uk/

4   Make notes on:

- the different sizes, kinds and colours of print

- the pictures, map and logo

- anything else you think is important about the presentation.

5   Look back to the example of writing about presentational devices that
is given on page 22.

Now write about the presentational devices used in 'The Wensleydale
Experience' and say what is important about them.

Looking at language

Writers use words in many different ways to create particular effects.

Questions

Sometimes they ask questions in order to make the reader think:

ARE MEN *afraid* OF **women's magazines?**

You

Do first children get a fair share of Dad?

You

Repetition

Sometimes they repeat a particular word or phrase (group of words) for emphasis:

FACT: nearly one in three 14 to 16-year-olds has taken drugs.

FACT: girls under 16 are smoking more cigarettes and taking higher quantities of drugs than boys of the same age.

FACT: one girl dies every month from sniffing solvents.

Sugar Magazine

For the most relaxing country cottage holidays, start with the most relaxing countries.

Exaggeration

Sometimes writers exaggerate in order to make something sound really good or really bad:

Mega Fantastic Best Ever Sale Starts Saturday!

This is probably **the** worst film you could see this year. Marks for entertainment value – 0. Boredom rating – a massive, not to be beaten, 10 out of 10.

Emotive language

Sometimes they use words or phrases to make the reader feel a particular emotion:

Throughout the developing world and Eastern Europe to help bring healthcare, education and eventual self-sufficiency

-denominational registered charity working with locally owned, long term projects

For Lidia, life began on the scrap heap...

The scrap heap on the outskirts of Lidia's home town in Bolivia is not a place you would want to visit. If the <u>foul stench</u> doesn't stop you in your tracks then the sight of the hundreds of rats and the <u>putrid waste</u> would be enough to <u>turn any stomach</u>.

<u>Unbelievable</u> as it may seem, this scrap heap, like so many others worldwide, has become home for thousands of families who live in <u>appalling poverty</u>, surviving by <u>scavenging for bits of food</u> to eat and the few scrap items they can sell on the streets.

CHRISTIAN CHILDREN'S FUND

The words that are underlined are intended to shock and to make the reader feel pity for these children. The word 'unbelievable', for example, suggests that the situation is so bad for these children it is hard to believe it is true. This is called *emotive language* because the writer is trying to influence the emotions of the reader.

ACTIVITY 1

Copy out the following sentences and underline the **emotive** words in them. There may be more than one word in each sentence.

- War, of any kind, involves a pitiful waste of lives.
- The drugs threat to Britain has now reached crisis point.
- The group's victorious tour of America ended with a mind-blowing concert in New York.

Now explain the effects of the words you have underlined.

Looking at the effects of language

When looking at a writer's use of language you need to consider:

- the words that are being used
- the effect that they are intended to have on the reader.

Read the following charity appeal. Try to work out what it is about and who it is written for.

headline clearly states aim of appeal

word 'mate' makes it sound informal and friendly

question invites reader to become involved

an informal way of asking what something is about

emotive language to make the reader feel sorry for the bears

a list of facts to emphasize how bad things are

SETTING FREE
THE BEARS

Instead of buying your mate/mum/ boyfriend a fluffy teddy for Christmas, why not adopt a real live bear cub? You'll be helping to save it from a terrible plight...

what's the story?
Earlier this year, members of the World Society For The Protection of Animals found a group of bear cubs wandering the streets of Istanbul. They took the frightened animals to their sanctuary in south-eastern Turkey, which they now share with 40 other rescued bears.
If the poor things *hadn't* been found, they'd have forcibly had their noses pierced and their teeth and claws removed, to live a miserable life as dancing bears to entertain the tourists. Thanks to the WSPA, there are no dancing bears in Turkey today, but there are still 8,000 bears being treated cruelly in other parts of the world, and for the past six years, the WSPA have been fighting to save bears *everywhere* from neglect and cruelty.
Projects are currently running to protect:
- Pandas – the most endangered bears, with only a measly 1,000 still alive.
- Spectacle bears – killed in South America because they're seen as pests.

- Sloth bears – used in bear baiting, where they're chased and killed by dogs.

over to you
By adopting a bear, you'll be directly contributing to the work of the WSPA Libearty campaign, which fights to save bears everywhere. For £15 you'll bag piccies, the story of your bear's life so far and an adoption certificate.
The money you give to the adoption scheme goes back into caring for your new family member and funding other WSPA campaigns. Plans are underway at this very mo' to build a special nursery next to the bear sanctuary in Turkey where the cubs can grow up in comfort. The WSPA needs your help and support to do this, so they can keep on working for happy bears everywhere.

and there's more...
The WSPA catalogue is brimming with nifty gift ideas like calendars, sweets and T-shirts – which all make great presents too!
For more adoption info contact: WSPA, 2 Langley Lane, London, SW8 1TJ (phone: 07000 214 214). For a catalogue phone 01209 831 831. Sorted!

a play on the word 'liberty', meaning freedom

slang, used to appeal to teenagers

makes it sound like a happy ending

emphasizes the number of good ideas

short for information to make it sound less formal

informal language again used to appeal to teenagers

SUGAR MAGAZINE

Now read the appeal again. Use the notes around the text to help you understand how the writer is using words to influence the reader.

How the writer uses language

Questions in the exam often ask you to write about how the writer uses language. When answering these questions you need to think about:

● words being used in a particular way

● the effect the words have on the reader

● how successful you think the writer has been.

This is an example of how you could start to write about the way words are used in the charity leaflet:

> The heading 'Setting Free the Bears' tells the reader what the appeal is about. The question 'why not adopt a real live bear cub?' makes the reader think about how s/he can help. The reader is addressed directly throughout the appeal with the use of 'you'. The language is informal and uses the kinds of expressions that teenagers might use. Instead of 'your friend' it uses 'your mate' and instead of asking 'what is it about?' it asks 'what's the story?'

ACTIVITY 2

The following sentences are also about the way words are used in the charity appeal text on the previous page. Copy them out and fill in the gaps, using the notes around the text to help you.

1 The writer uses emotive words such as _____ and_____ . These are intended to make the reader feel _____ .

2 The facts are given in the form of _____. This emphasizes how _____ .

3 Bears are linked to freedom with the play on the word 'liberty'. The new word _____ suggests both bears and freedom.

4 Some examples of words being used to appeal to teenagers are _____ and _____ .

ACTIVITY 3

Once you have thought carefully about the words in the appeal text you need to think about the effect the whole thing has on the reader. Which of the following statements do you agree with? Give your reasons.

● It involves the reader by using the word 'you'.

● It uses the kind of words that teenagers would identify with.

● It uses emotive words that make the reader feel sorry for the bears.

● It answers questions that make the reader think.

● It makes the reader believe that adopting a bear will make a difference.

Try to add more statements of your own.

Persuasive language

Holiday brochures have two main purposes:

● they aim to interest the reader and make him/her want to go to a particular place

● they aim to persuade the reader to choose that holiday rather than another one.

Read the following extract from a Butlin's brochure. The words in this passage
are carefully chosen to make both the holiday and the company sound good.

A family holiday at Butlin's is <u>a must</u> for 1998. We've <u>pulled out all the stops</u> this year to make it a <u>holiday to remember</u>. There are sub-tropical waterworlds, with <u>a full range</u> of flumes and water rides. For the sports enthusiast, there's <u>every kind of activity</u>, from 1998 World Cup celebrations to basketball. For <u>some real exhilaration</u>, our funfairs are <u>full of thrilling rides</u> for everyone, from toddlers to adults. We'll make sure no one will be left out of <u>a memorable holiday</u> at Butlin's.

The underlined words are being used to influence and persuade the reader.

ACTIVITY 4

Copy out the following table. In the left-hand column list the underlined words. In the right-hand column write the message behind the words. The first three are done for you.

UNDERLINED WORDS	WHAT THEY'RE REALLY SAYING
a must	This holiday shouldn't be missed.
pulled out all the stops	We've done everything we can to make this a good holiday.
a holiday to remember	This holiday will be so good you'll want to remember it.

ACTIVITY 5

Read the following extract from the same brochure:

It's what we're famous for, superb entertainment from dawn to dusk until late.

There's entertainment for the children at their own special clubs and superb late night cabaret for adults. Teenagers too have their own club activities and discos. Alternatively, you can all get together at one of our great family shows where the blend of music, magic and laughter is guaranteed to keep everyone happy.

But if you just prefer to relax, a warm welcome awaits you in any of our bars and restaurants.

The choice is yours!

Copy out this text. Underline the words and phrases that you think are being used to persuade the reader. What is the message behind each of the words and phrases you have selected? Organize your answers in table form as you did for Activity 4.

Test yourself

Read the following extract from a different holiday brochure.

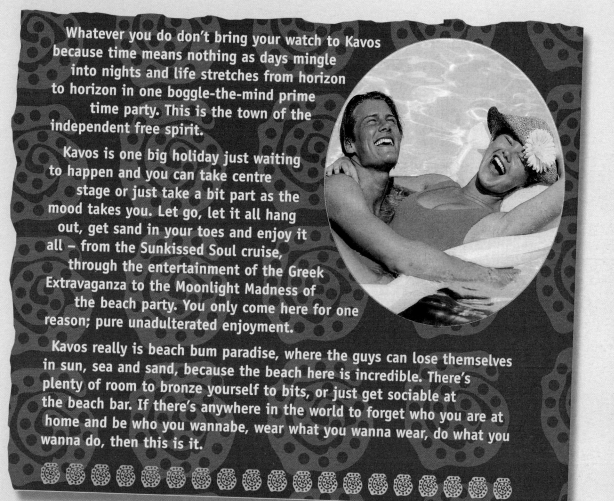

Whatever you do don't bring your watch to Kavos because time means nothing as days mingle into nights and life stretches from horizon to horizon in one boggle-the-mind prime time party. This is the town of the independent free spirit.

Kavos is one big holiday just waiting to happen and you can take centre stage or just take a bit part as the mood takes you. Let go, let it all hang out, get sand in your toes and enjoy it all – from the Sunkissed Soul cruise, through the entertainment of the Greek Extravaganza to the Moonlight Madness of the beach party. You only come here for one reason; pure unadulterated enjoyment.

Kavos really is beach bum paradise, where the guys can lose themselves in sun, sea and sand, because the beach here is incredible. There's plenty of room to bronze yourself to bits, or just get sociable at the beach bar. If there's anywhere in the world to forget who you are at home and be who you wannabe, wear what you wanna wear, do what you wanna do, then this is it.

1 Does the text address the reader directly? How do you know? What effect does this have?

2 The following phrases are taken from the first paragraph. What do they suggest to you? How would you explain their meaning?

- time means nothing

- boggle-the-mind prime time party

- the independent free spirit.

3 Reread the second paragraph. How does the writer make Kavos sound like a good holiday place? Pick out words and phrases that help to achieve this.

4 Reread the last sentence. How does the writer use repetition? What is the effect of this?

5 Phrases such as *boggle-the-mind* and *let it all hang out* are examples of the writer using language informally. List any other examples you can find.

6 Read your answers to questions 1–5. Put your ideas together and write a paragraph about the writer's use of language in this extract.

Choosing the right material

Scanning

You don't always need to read every single detail in a text. For example, when you read a timetable your eyes move quickly over the text until they find the right bits of information. This process is known as *scanning*. Improving your skills in scanning will help you to pick out the information from a text in order to answer a particular question.

Look at the extract below from a leisure centre guide. See how quickly you can find the answers to the questions in Activity 1 on page 33.

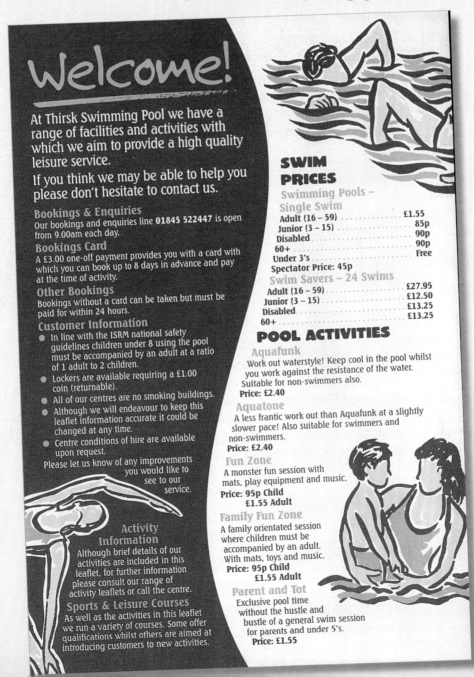

Welcome!

At Thirsk Swimming Pool we have a range of facilities and activities with which we aim to provide a high quality leisure service.

If you think we may be able to help you please don't hesitate to contact us.

Bookings & Enquiries
Our bookings and enquiries line **01845 522447** is open from 9.00am each day.

Bookings Card
A £3.00 one-off payment provides you with a card with which you can book up to 8 days in advance and pay at the time of activity.

Other Bookings
Bookings without a card can be taken but must be paid for within 24 hours.

Customer Information
- In line with the ISRM national safety guidelines children under 8 using the pool must be accompanied by an adult at a ratio of 1 adult to 2 children.
- Lockers are available requiring a £1.00 coin (returnable).
- All of our centres are no smoking buildings.
- Although we will endeavour to keep this leaflet information accurate it could be changed at any time.
- Centre conditions of hire are available upon request.

Please let us know of any improvements you would like to see to our service.

Activity Information
Although brief details of our activities are included in this leaflet, for further information please consult our range of activity leaflets or call the centre.

Sports & Leisure Courses
As well as the activities in this leaflet we run a variety of courses. Some offer qualifications whilst others are aimed at introducing customers to new activities.

SWIM PRICES

Swimming Pools – Single Swim

Adult (16 – 59)	£1.55
Junior (3 – 15)	85p
Disabled	90p
60+	90p
Under 3's	Free
Spectator Price: 45p	

Swim Savers – 24 Swims

Adult (16 – 59)	£27.95
Junior (3 – 15)	£12.50
Disabled	£13.25
60+	£13.25

POOL ACTIVITIES

Aquafunk
Work out waterstyle! Keep cool in the pool whilst you work against the resistance of the water. Suitable for non-swimmers also.
Price: £2.40

Aquatone
A less frantic work out than Aquafunk at a slightly slower pace! Also suitable for swimmers and non-swimmers.
Price: £2.40

Fun Zone
A monster fun session with mats, play equipment and music.
Price: 95p Child
£1.55 Adult

Family Fun Zone
A family orientated session where children must be accompanied by an adult. With mats, toys and music.
Price: 95p Child
£1.55 Adult

Parent and Tot
Exclusive pool time without the hustle and bustle of a general swim session for parents and under 5's.
Price: £1.55

ACTIVITY 1

- How much does it cost an adult to swim?
- What would you find at the pool during Fun Zone times?
- Are you allowed to smoke in the leisure centre?

Sports Unlimited

CenterParcs

An unrivalled range of indoor and outdoor sports.

You're here to unwind and we have all your favourite ways of doing it. At Center Parcs the appeal is not just the vast choice of sporting activities but the exhilarating environment you do them in, whether indoors in the Jardin des Sports or the Country Club or outside on our superb courts, cycle paths and trim trails.

Families love it because it's a chance either to play a sport together or to pursue their own interests – something it's often too complicated to do at home. Couples love it because the sports activities are spread over such a wide area that they never feel crowded out by children's interests. For everyone it's a chance to try new sports, specialist sports and team sports, with expert help and tuition.

Most activities can be booked one day in advance from the moment you arrive, at Leisure Booking Points across the Village. Bookings are generally by the hour and half-hour and you'll find that prices are competitive with most leisure centres. To give you some examples of typical costs, an hour of T'ai Chi or windsurfing would cost around £4.00 each. Playing Adventure/Crazy Golf would cost adults £2.20 and children £1.50. A soccer school session costs around £6.00, a weekend pass to the Fitness Room around £5.50 and a two-hour Kindergarten session or a Ranger's Ramble around £5.00.

Our adventure playgrounds and indoor play areas are great fun for all children, and in the Kindergarten you'll find everything from puppet making to face painting. Take advantage of our babysitting service, available throughout the day and evening, when you want to book a game of something on your own. We really do want you to relax.

ACTIVITY 2

Look at this extract from a guide to Center Parcs. This time there are no sub-headings to help you. Time how long it takes you to find the answers to these questions.

- What is the cost of a soccer school session?
- Where do you go to book activities?
- Why, according to the extract, do couples love to go there?
- What would you find in the Kindergarten?

Skimming

So far you have *scanned* the texts in order to find particular details. Sometimes, however, we need to read the whole of a text quickly in order to get a general idea of what it is about. This is known as *skim-reading*.

ACTIVITY 3

Read the following text as quickly as you can. The key points have been underlined for you. Once you have read the whole text, close your book and write down what it was about. How many details can you remember?

Kickboxing/Mua Thai

Historians may one day know why kicking people in the head has become so underline popular in the late '90s. For the moment we can only gaze in wonder at the popularity of underline kickboxing and the more brutal Mua Thai (Thaiboxing). Nearly a quarter of all martial arts fans in Britain have taken up these two forms.

'underline Kickboxing is easier to learn because you're not using elbows and knees to fight, and don't need to master locks, holds and throws,' says London instructor, Billy Judd. 'You underline become extremely fit very quickly,' he says. 'Lots of people want to stay fit and learn self-defence too.'

Most clubs offer underline beginner classes in both of these sports. A underline thorough medical examination is advised before beginning. Once you start sparring you will need a underline gum shield and a underline set of hand wraps.

If, however, you want to avoid getting well and truly thumped you could join a underline kickbox aerobic class. These offer similar types of moves, without the punches, and are usually underline on offer at most fitness centres.

MEN'S HEALTH

ACTIVITY 4

Read the following text as quickly as you can. This time the key points have not been underlined. Once you have read the whole text, close your book and write down what it was about. How many details can you remember?

AS A LONE FEMALE TRAVELLING HOME LATE FROM WORK, safety is an issue. I'd like to think I could defend myself if I needed to. So karate seemed like a good idea and I signed up for a class at the Coulsdon Martial Arts Centre, in Surrey.

I turned up and found I was in a mixed-ability class. I was wearing a bright purple tracksuit and everyone around me was in snow white 'gi' (pronounced *ghee*) suits. The class was small: just 12 people – a fellow 'white belt', then all the colours of the rainbow up to instructor Patrick Walsh's black belt. I was surprised to see teenagers partnering the middle-aged. They had one thing in common though – enthusiasm.

The class was very supportive and by the end of the evening I felt both calm and exhilarated. It's quite odd, unlike anything I've ever tried but thoroughly enjoyable. After my hour and a quarter session I went home determined to practise my moves in readiness for the next week!

Looking across texts

Sometimes exam questions will ask you to think and write about more than one text. You may be asked to:

- use material from them in order to build a wider picture
- note points of similarity and difference between them.

To do this you need to be able to take different pieces of information from different texts and use them together.

Read the following article. It was written in response to government proposals to suspend the primary school curriculum for PE.

▼A

The slimming down of the curriculum for school children is a dangerous measure which threatens the long-term health of the nation,
5 according to the Central Council for Physical Recreation (CCPR).

The council claims it will leave children less fit than ever and will squeeze out swimming lessons
10 altogether. 'This will be seen as a reduction in PE by teachers,' said Nigel Hook, from the CCPR. 'It is not in the long-term interests of Britain, which requires a fit, healthy
15 workforce. Primary school is the most important time for developing a love of exercise.'

Research has shown that British children are becoming less active, he
20 said, while the number of children who have heart disease is rising.

The CCPR is particularly concerned about the future of swimming. 'There is nothing more
25 important in primary PE than swimming. The chances of teaching every child to swim will be nil. Mums and Dads should be going barmy about this,' said Mr Hook.
30 Meanwhile, the Physical Education Association (PEA) argues that British children already take less exercise than most European children at only 90 minutes a week.
35 It is campaigning for a two-hour minimum.

TIMES EDUCATIONAL SUPPLEMENT

ACTIVITY 5

Here is a list of the key points of this article.

- CCPR says the slimming down of the curriculum threatens the nation's health.
- Children will be less fit and there will be no swimming lessons.
- Primary school is where children learn to love exercise.
- Children are becoming less active and heart disease is on the rise.
- PEA wants at least two hours' exercise per week.

Find these key points and write down the numbers of the lines where they appear.

Now read this article, written by a sixteen-year-old, which also argues that more, not less, sport is needed in schools.

B ▶ **: Give us a Sporting Chance**

According to a recent government report, 72% of teenagers do less than the recommended two hours of sport in school per week. It seems the only exercise teenagers now get is pressing the remote control for the telly. They are becoming unfit, lazy and overweight. Because of this, doctors are already predicting a huge rise in the number of people with heart disease. The health and fitness of the nation is now at stake.

At the moment few people like doing PE in schools. Who wants to stand on a muddy field in the freezing cold carrying an oddly shaped piece of wood or kicking a piece of leather? Outdated showers that only spray iced water are the final straw! But it needn't be like this. Sport in schools, *all* schools, can be exciting and worthwhile. It can offer choice and set a healthy pattern for adult life.

The French, Germans and Spanish do on average 3 hours of sport per week. They have all the latest equipment, including sports centres and indoor pitches, while we are left with outdated rubbish. Against competition like this what chance is there for our future national teams? PE conditions and facilities must be improved to European standards *now*, before it's too late.

VICTOR RUSHTON

ACTIVITY 6

1 List the key points in this article.

2 Compare the list of key points for Article B with the list of key points for Article A. Which points are similar? Which points are different?

3 Once you have worked out the answers to these questions you are ready to put your ideas into sentences. Complete the following, choosing your words from the list in the box below:

Article A is mainly about sport in primary schools whereas Article B is about sport in _____ schools.

Both articles claim that less sport means more problems with _____ disease.

Swimming is given a lot of importance in _____ but is not mentioned in _____ .

Article A argues that more time for sport is important. Article B agrees with this but also argues for better _____ .

money   secondary   equipment   Article A   heart   Article B

4 Now write some sentences of your own showing other similarities and differences between the texts.

Test yourself

Read the texts on this page and page 38, then answer these questions.

1 What is health?

2 Give one example of **a)** mental well-being **b)** social well-being.

3 How could a car accident affect your social well-being?

4 What indoor sports are recommended to Rachel Thompson?

5 Who can eat a high-fat diet and still stay slim?

6 What exercise is good for flexibility and relaxation?

7 Which **two** texts do you feel give you the most helpful information about keeping fit? Give three clear reasons for each of your choices.

What is health?

Health doesn't just mean the absence of sickness. **Health is a state of complete physical, mental and social well-being.** It means you feel good all round.

Physical well-being   Physical well-being means:

- your heart, lungs and other body systems are working well
- you have no illnesses or injuries.

Mental well-being   Mental well-being means:

- you are able to cope with stress – for example when you run into problems, or have to work very hard before exams
- you are able to control your emotions; even if you feel very angry you don't get violent
- you feel positive about yourself; you know you are okay as a person. You have **self-esteem**.

Social well-being   Social well-being means:

- you have enough to eat, and clothing and shelter; these are the most basic human needs
- you have friendship and support
- you feel you have some value in society, whether it is in school, in a job or in your family.

These kinds of well-being are all related. If you get injured in a car accident it may affect your mental well-being. It may also affect your social well-being, if you can't work and lose touch with your friends.

PE TO 16

Work it, girl!

If you've had a slobbed-out o... ...to get going again. But if you're thinking of joining... exercise class, then make sure you get the right one, so you don't bust your guts too soon!

Exercise	Good for	What you have to do
Aerobics	Heart and lungs	Dance like a maniac and get toned up
Step	Heart, lungs, legs and bum	Like aerobics but you step on/off a block
Slide	Thighs, heart and lungs	Glide about on a board – very hard work!
Body Sculpting	Everywhere	Uses weights to tone up muscles
Circuit Training	Complete calorie burner	Loads of different exercises
Yoga	Flexibility and relaxation	Stretches and breathing control
Box Aerobics	Everything!	Boxing stuff...

BLISS MAGAZINE

Q I spend a lot of time in the gym working out either on the rowing machine or treadmill, plus I normally jog first thing most mornings. I love exercising and I feel better for it, but now the weather has changed I don't feel like dragging myself outside. How can I keep up my enthusiasm?
Rachel Thompson

A Trying a different activity is always a great way to revitalize and remotivate. As an added benefit you may find that your current fitness levels improve too. If you don't fancy braving the weather for a while, what about an indoor sport like basketball, volleyball or any of the studio-based classes that come under the aerobic umbrella, like Body Pump or Spinning? Racquet sports like squash or badminton are great exercise, too. Phone around and find out what's available in your area, then keep trying until you find something you enjoy.

As you usually work out alone, see if you can arrange an exercise partner – training with a buddy can be fun and the fact that someone is expecting you can help to motivate you to make all your scheduled sessions.

TEE DOBINSON

Eat fat stay slim

Want to eat a diet that consists mainly of doughnuts and beer? Become a professional athlete. That's the message from studies in both America and South Africa, which have shown that not only will an athlete stay slim on a diet of up to 43 per cent fat, but that his performance might also improve. Unfortunately mere mortals are unable to expend the calories in the way endurance athletes can, so it's brown rice and vegetables for the rest of us.

Homer Simpson:
'a doughnut a day makes me a bloater.'

MEN'S HEALTH

Reading Poetry

For your GCSE examination in English you will be studying the work of at least one poet in the English literary tradition and some poems from other cultures and traditions. These poems are contained in your **NEAB Anthology.**

In the examination you will be asked to show that you know what the poems are about, that you understand how the poet is putting words together to create a particular effect, and that you have thought carefully about the effect the poem has on you.

In order to answer the questions on poetry in your examination you need to learn to study poems in particular ways. This section uses a variety of poems from different times and places to teach you the skills you need to use when reading the poems in your **Anthology.** It does *not* use poems from a specific anthology (NEAB will change its **Anthology** every two or three years). When you have completed this section you should use the skills you have learned to help you study your **Anthology** poems.

In this section you will be shown how to:

- read for meaning
- think about presentation
- look at language
- choose the right material.

Reading of poetry is tested in NEAB GCSE English, Paper 2 Section A.

Thinking about meaning

Once you have read a poem through a couple of times the first question you need to ask is, 'What is it about?' Don't worry if you can't answer the question straight away. It may take several attempts before you understand what is being said. Often, the more times you read a poem the more layers of meanings you will find in it.

First impressions

Read the following poem aloud several times. As you are reading, decide where you need to pause to make sense of it and think about what tone of voice you should use. When you have done this, write down what you think it is about.

The Road Not Taken

Two roads diverged in a yellow wood,
And sorry I could not travel both
And be one traveller, long I stood
And looked down one as far as I could
5 To where it bent in the undergrowth;

Then took the other, as just as fair,
And having perhaps the better claim,
Because it was grassy and wanted wear;
Though as for that the passing there
10 Had worn them really about the same.

And both that morning equally lay
In leaves no step had trodden black.
Oh, I kept the first for another day!
Yet knowing how way leads on to way,
15 I doubted if I should ever come back.

I shall be telling this with a sigh
Somewhere ages and ages hence;
Two roads diverged in a wood, and I –
I took the one less travelled by,
20 And that has made all the diference.

Robert Frost

ACTIVITY 1

Now you are going to work out the meaning in more detail. Firstly you need to think carefully about each verse or stanza of the poem.

First verse, lines 1–5

1   What is the meaning of *diverged*?

2   What choice does the poet have to make?

3   What would the poet like to do?

4   How far can he see along the road he looks down?

Second verse, lines 6–10

5   Why does he take the other road?

6   Is there really any difference between the appearance of the roads?

Third verse, lines 11–15

7   Has anyone travelled along either of the roads that morning?

8   Why does he doubt that he will ever come back?

Fourth verse, lines 16–20

9   What scene does the poet imagine in the future?

10 What do you think is meant by the final line of the poem?

So far you have thought about the surface meaning of the poem. On the surface this poem is about a traveller and how his decision to take one road rather than another made a difference to his life.

ACTIVITY 2

Now you need to explore the other things the poet could be saying. You need to think about what the roads might represent or symbolize.

1   Think about the choices you have to make in life. At the moment you are probably starting to think about what you will do when you leave school. Suppose you have to decide whether to start work or go to college. You want to do both but that's impossible.

    To what extent is the traveller's choice about the roads the same as the choice you have to make?

2   Suppose you make the choice to start work thinking that you might still go back to college at a later date. Read lines 13–15 again. What does the poet seem to be saying about this?

3   Think ahead to the future and the effects your choice to start work might have on your life. In what ways could this choice make *all the difference*?

Throughout our lives we all have to make important choices to do with work, love, children and how we live our lives. Think about these choices and then read the poem again carefully. What do you think Robert Frost is saying about these choices?

ACTIVITY 3

Now that you have started to explore the ideas in the poem you are ready to think again about the meaning of particular words and phrases.

1 Why do you think the poet chose to write about *a yellow wood*? What does the colour yellow suggest to you?

2 *And looked down one as far as I could*
   To where it bent in the undergrowth;
   What is Frost saying about the road he looks down? What does this suggest about the *roads* we follow in life?

3 Which line in the poem suggests that there is no real difference between the roads?

4 What do you now understand by the words:
   Yet knowing how way leads on to way,

5 The poet says he will be *telling this with a sigh*. What does this suggest about his feelings towards the choices he has made?

6 Why do you think Frost called his poem **The Road Not Taken**?

What is this poem about?

Now that you have thought carefully about the poem you are ready to answer this question. Look back over your answers to the questions in Activities 1–3. Organize your ideas under two sub-headings:

- surface meaning
- ideas beneath the surface.

Now write two paragraphs about the meaning of the poem. You might find it helpful to start your paragraphs in the following ways:

1 On the surface **The Road Not Taken** seems to be about ...

2 Having studied the poem more carefully I can find other meanings in it.

Referring to the poem

When you write about poetry you need to refer to the poem itself. Sometimes you will want to refer to things in the poem without quoting directly from it. For example:

The poet, Robert Frost, writes about himself as a traveller who has to make a choice between two roads. He spends a long time deciding which one to take.

At other times you will want to make closer reference to the poem by quoting directly from it. You need to pick out words or phrases from the poem to support the points you are making. For example:

● He looked down one road which 'bent in the undergrowth'.

● He finally took the other one simply because 'it was grassy and wanted wear'.

Notice how the quotation marks are placed before and after the words that are taken directly from the poem.

Sometimes you will want to quote whole lines from the poem. These examples show you how to do this:

● Though the poet does finally choose one of the roads he realizes there is very little difference between them:
'Though as for that the passing there
Had worn them really about the same.'

● The poet realizes he is unlikely to ever get the opportunity to follow the road he did not choose:
'Yet knowing how way leads on to way,
I doubted if I should ever come back.'

Notice how the lines of poetry are set on separate lines, as they are written in the poem. A colon : is used to show that the quotation is to follow.

ACTIVITY 4

Complete the following sentences using suitable words or phrases from **The Road Not Taken**:

● The poet would like to choose both roads and be '_____'.

● He chose the one he did because it perhaps had '_____'.

Now complete the following, putting the quotation marks in yourself.

● The poet doubts he will ever come back because he knows how _____.

● When he is older he will be telling this story with _____.

Now complete the following by putting in the colons and quotation marks:

He makes it clear that there is nothing that makes the one road more attractive than the other And both that morning equally lay In leaves no step had trodden black. There is a note of regret and sadness in his voice when he says I took the one less travelled by, And that has made all the difference.

Poems from other cultures and traditions

People from all races and countries write poetry. Sometimes you will come across poems that describe things that are unfamiliar to you. They may be set in another country or refer to events in another race's history. They may describe situations that you find unusual. They may express ideas in a way that you have not come across before.

When you are reading and writing about poems like this, as well as understanding what they are about, you need to be able to say what is different about them.

First impressions

Read the poem on page 45 aloud several times. As you are reading, decide where you need to pause to make sense of it and think about what is the best voice to read it in. When you have done this, write down what you think it is about.

ACTIVITY 5

Now you are going to work out the meaning in more detail by thinking carefully about each verse of the poem.

First verse, lines 1–10

1 What happens when the sound of the conch is heard?

2 What is the canoe made from?

3 Copy out this sentence and fill in the missing words:
   It is being carried from up _____ down to the _____.

4 Who is carrying the canoe?

5 How do you think the mothers and children are feeling?

Second verse, lines 11–20

6 What happens when the sound of the conch is heard?

7 Why was the conch sounded?

8 What was in the canoes?

9 What does the word 'loaded' in line 16 suggest to you?

10 How do you think the mothers and children are feeling?

Third verse, lines 21–30

11 What happens when the conch is heard this time?

12 What has happened?

13 What are the mothers and children staring at?

14 How do you think the mothers and children are feeling now?

Song of the Sea and People

Shell of the conch* was sounded,
sounded like foghorn.
Women rushed to doorways,
to fences, to gateways, and watched.
5 Canoe made from cotton tree
came sailing shoulder high, from up
mountain-pass down to the sea.
      They stared
      at many men under canoe.
10   The mothers and children stared.

Shell of the conch was sounded,
sounded like foghorn.
Women rushed to seaside.
Canoes had come in,
15 come in from way out
of big sea, loaded
with fish, crabs and lobsters.
      They stared
      at sea-catch.
20   The mothers and children stared.

Shell of the conch was sounded,
sounded like foghorn.
Women rushed to seaside.
Canoe out of cotton tree had thrown men,
25 thrown them into deep sea.
Deep sea swallowed men.
Big sea got boat back.
      They stared
      at empty canoe.
30   The mothers and children stared.

James Berry

*A conch is the shell of a kind of shellfish.
It is sometimes used as a horn.

What is this poem about?

To answer this question you need to link your ideas from Activity 5 together.
Your answer might be something like this:

The poem starts with the sound of a conch shell. On hearing this the women rush out of their homes to see what is happening. They stare at the men carrying a canoe, made from the wood of a cotton tree, from the 'mountain pass down to the sea'. They probably feel very proud at what the men have done. In the second verse the conch shell is blown again and again the women rush out. This time they go to the sea and watch the canoes come in filled with fish. They probably feel very pleased that the fishing trip has been successful. The third verse also starts with the sound of the conch shell. Again the women rush to the sea shore. This time the canoe is empty. The men who were in it have been drowned. The women and children stare, this time feeling huge sadness at the loss of their husbands and fathers. Perhaps they are also remembering how they had felt at other, happier times.

ACTIVITY 6

Think about what makes this poem different. What details tell you something about the people's culture? Now try to answer these questions.

1   What kind of shell is used to sound the warning? Where might you find such a shell?

2   What do you learn about the place where these people live?

3   What do the men do?

4   Is there anything unusual about the way the words are put together that would make you think this poem is from another culture? Give examples from the poem.

Test yourself

Read through the following poem several times.

But you didn't

Remember the time you lent me your car and I dented it?
I thought you'd kill me …
But you didn't.

Remember the time I forgot to tell you the dance was
5 formal, and you came in jeans?
I thought you'd hate me …
But you didn't.

Remember the times I'd flirt with
other boys just to make you jealous, and
10 you were?
I thought you'd drop me …
But you didn't.

There were plenty of things you did to put up with me,
to keep me happy, to love me, and there are
15 so many things I wanted to tell
you when you returned from
Vietnam …
But you didn't.

Merrill Glass

> Vietnam is in Southeast
> Asia. Between 1965 and
> 1973 the United States of
> America was at war with
> Vietnam. Many thousands of
> lives were lost on both sides
> in the conflict. Many
> Americans were opposed to
> their country's participation.

Now answer these questions.

1 What had the woman done in the first verse?

2 How did she expect the other person to react?

3 What had she done in the second verse?

4 How did she expect the other person to react?

5 Why did she flirt with other boys?

6 What did she think might happen?

7 Look through the first three verses again. What kind of person do you think her boyfriend was? What words would you use to describe him?

8 What does she appreciate about him in verse four?

9 What did she want to do when he returned from Vietnam?

10 What happened in Vietnam? Use the notes at the side of the poem to help you answer this.

11 What do you think happened to him?

12 How do you think the woman feels about her lost love?

13 Who is the poem written for?

Now that you have thought about the poem carefully you are ready to answer the question **'What is this poem about?'** Remember to link your ideas together.

Thinking about presentation

How can you tell at first glance that a piece of writing is a poem and not a prose passage?

Look at the following two texts. They are both, in different ways, about cruelty to dogs. One is a poem and one is a prose passage.

The Dog Lovers

So they bought you
And kept you in a
Very good home,
Central heating
5 TV
A deep freeze
A *very* good home –
No one to take you
For that lovely long run –
10 But otherwise
'A *very* good home'.
They fed you Pal and Chum
But not that lovely long run,
Until, mad with energy and boredom
15 You escaped – and ran and ran and ran
Under a car.
Today they will cry for you –
Tomorrow they will buy another dog.

Spike Milligan

Stray dogs on increase

DOZENS of dogs have been abandoned on Britain's streets over Christmas, animal lovers said last night.

The number of strays arriving at the country's leading home for abandoned dogs has increased steadily since Christmas Eve.

Staff are working around the clock to care for unwanted Christmas pets at Battersea Dogs' Home, in south London, which has taken in 33 animals left to roam the city's streets over the past three days – eight per cent more than last year. A total of 706 abandoned dogs are at the centre, and spokesman Stephen Danos said he expects this figure to increase over the festive season.

He said: 'What is worrying is that if the number of stray dogs in the home is up now, just a few days into Christmas, what will it be like in late January?'

The 137-year-old sanctuary for abandoned dogs saw nine arrivals on Christmas Eve, a dozen more on Christmas Day, and another dozen by mid-afternoon yesterday.

List the ways in which the two texts *look* different.

Northern Echo

First impressions

Read the poem aloud. Experiment with pausing in different places. Which words should you give most emphasis to? What tone of voice should you use? Should this change for different parts of the poem?

Form

When we talk about the way a poem is set out on the page and the way the words are put together we are talking about the poem's **form**. Form is an important feature of poetry. In order to write about the form of a poem you need to think about what the poet is trying to achieve in setting his words out in this particular way.

ACTIVITY 1

Think about the ways the words in the poem have been set out on the page. Find examples of the following:

- lines that are not the same length
- lines that end in the same word
- lines that end with a dash (like this –)
- words that are not written in sentences
- phrases (groups of words) that are repeated.

What is the effect of these features?

Repetition

Poets often use *repetition*. Sometimes they use it for emphasis – to make sure the reader gets the message. There is a lot of repetition in **The Dog Lovers**.

ACTIVITY 2

1 How many times does the word *you* appear in the poem?

2 Who is the *you* referring to?

3 How many times does the phrase *a very good home* appear in the poem?

4 Did the dog have a very good home? Give reasons for your answer.

5 How many times does the phrase *that lovely long run* appear in the poem? What is important about this phrase?

6 Look at the line that ends *and ran and ran and ran.* Why are these words repeated?

7 What message do you think Spike Milligan is trying to get across to his readers in this poem?

Poetry is intended to be read aloud and not simply seen on a page. It is the only way to hear the sounds of the words and the patterns of sound that are such an important part of poetry. It is through listening to poetry and reading it aloud that we start to:

● hear the *rhymes*

● feel the *rhythm* of the words.

Rhyme

Words *rhyme* when they end with the same sound.

ACTIVITY 3

Pick out and write down the rhyming pairs of words from the box below:

> trick tell day trees might pick kite
> fail sees wood tray shell could trail

Now try and think of words that rhyme with the following:

● hand

● train

● calls

● tame

● slow.

Look at and read the following poem. It is written in *rhyming couplets.*
These are two lines where the word at the end of the first line rhymes with
the word at the end of the second line. Think about where you should pause
and how you should read the poem for greatest effect.

The Bat

By day the bat is cousin to the mouse.
He likes the attic of an aging house.

His fingers make a hat about his head.
His pulse beat is so slow we think him dead.

5 He loops in crazy figures half the night
Among the trees that face the corner light.

But when he brushes up against a screen,
We are afraid of what our eyes have seen:

For something is amiss or out of place
10 When mice with wings can wear a human face.

Theodore Roethke

ACTIVITY 4

Now answer the following questions.

1 Where do you need to pause to make sense of the poem?

2 What does each separate couplet tell you about the bat? How are these
different ideas brought together in the last couplet?

Notice how the rhymes help to link words *and* ideas in this poem.

Not all poems rhyme, though many poems contain rhyme *within* the lines as well as at the end of them.

Read the following extracts from three different poems, then do Activity 5.

a   Love is the presents in Christmas shops
       Love is when you're feeling Top of the Pops
       Love is what happens when the music stops
       Love is

       Adrian Henri

b   The sand is grey, but clean.
       The seagulls play
       at the water's edge, with
       fingery feet.

       Olga Benjamin

c   Once upon a midnight dreary, while I pondered, weak and weary,
       Over many a quaint and curious volume of forgotten lore –
       While I nodded, nearly napping, suddenly there came a tapping,
       As of some one gently rapping, rapping at my chamber door.

       Edgar Allan Poe

ACTIVITY 5

Make a list of the words that rhyme in each of these extracts a, b and c. Remember – not all rhymes come at the end of lines.

Rhythm

The best way to understand *rhythm* is to think about beat. Rhythms are all around us. Think of the regular ticking of a clock, the rain against a window pane or the wheels of a train.

When thinking about poetry it is the beat of the words that is important and the pattern of sounds they make.

ACTIVITY 6

Syllables are the separate sounds in a word. For example yes/ter/day has three syllables. The beat of a line of poetry is made up of the number of syllables in the words and the number of words in a line.

Count the number of syllables in each line of **The Bat** (page 51). What do you notice? Now count the number of syllables in each line of extracts a, b and c on page 52. Write down what you discover about each poem.

The poem **Limbo**, on page 54, is about the slave trade and the terrible experiences of the slaves on the ships that were used to transport them from West Africa to the West Indies. The *rhythm* of the poem suggests the musical beat of the West Indian limbo dance. In this dance the dancer bends backwards to pass under a stick which is gradually lowered.

Read the poem through several times. Try tapping out the rhythm as you read it. How does the beat help to get across the idea of a dance?

Think about how the writer mixes ideas about the dance with the experiences of the slaves.

Limbo

And limbo stick is the silence in front of me
limbo

limbo
limbo like me
5 *limbo*
limbo like me

long dark night is the silence in front of me
limbo
limbo like me
10 stick hit sound
and the ship like it ready

stick hit sound
and the dark still steady

limbo
15 *limbo like me*

long dark deck and the water surrounding me
long dark deck and the silence is over me

limbo
limbo like me
20 stick is the whip
and the dark deck is slavery

stick is the whip
and the dark deck is slavery

limbo
25 *limbo like me*
drum stick knocks
and the darkness is over me

knees spread wide
and the water is hiding me

30 *limbo*
limbo like me
knees spread wide
and the dark ground is under me

down
35 down
down

and the drummer is calling me
limbo
limbo like me

40 sun coming up
and the drummers are praising me

out of the dark
and the dumb gods are raising me

up
45 up
up
and the music is saving me

hot
slow
50 step
on the limbo ground

Edward Kamau Brathwaite

ACTIVITY 7

Once you have read the poem a number of times make a list of the different words and phrases that are repeated. What do you think the poet achieves through this *repetition?*

Test *yourself*

Read the following poem aloud several times.

Nooligan

I'm a nooligan
dont give a toss
in our class
I'm the boss
5   (well, one of them)

I'm a nooligan
got a nard 'ead
step out of line
and youre dead
10   (well, bleedin)

I'm a nooligan
I spray me name
all over town
footballs me game
15   (well, watchin)

I'm a nooligan
violence is fun
gonna be a nassassin
or a nired gun
20   (well, a soldier)

Roger McGough

Now answer these questions.

1   How many verses are there? What do the first four lines of each verse tell you about the 'nooligan'?

2   What do you learn about the 'nooligan' from the last line of each verse? Why do you think these words are put in brackets?

3   Make a list of the words that rhyme in each of the verses.

4   Which line is repeated in every verse? Why do you think the writer has done this?

5   Count the number of syllables in each line. Is there a pattern?

6   Try memorizing the first verse of the poem. In what ways does the use of rhyme, rhythm and repetition make the poem as a whole easy to remember?

Looking at language

Poets use words in a variety of ways to achieve different effects.
If you are reading poetry you need to be able to:

- recognize what the poet is doing
- think and write about the ways the words work.

There are some obvious techniques that a poet may use to achieve
these effects, such as *simile* and *metaphor*.

It is helpful to use these names when you can, but the most
important thing is to be able to understand how the words are
being used and the effect they have.

Similes

A *simile* is the direct comparison of one thing with another,
as in the following example:

Clockface

Hours pass
slowly as a snail
creeping between the grassblades
of the minutes.

Judith Thurman

Think about a clockface and the hour and minute hands as they pass
across its surface. Now think about time and how it can pass quickly or
slowly. In this poem time is passing slowly, so slowly that it is like *a snail
creeping between the grassblades of the minutes*. Think about a snail and
how slowly it moves. The word *creeping* emphasizes this. Now think
about blades of grass and how close they are together. Yet here the poet
presents them as though they were entirely separate. So slowly does a
snail move that even blades of grass seem far apart. That's pretty slow
and that's how slowly time is passing for the poet. By using this image or
picture of a snail the poet helps us to feel what she is feeling.

ACTIVITY 1

Try writing your own short poem. Imagine you are on holiday and the time is passing very quickly. Think of the different images you could use to show your reader just how quickly time is passing. Start your poem with Hours pass quickly as a...

ACTIVITY 2

Now read the **similes** in the following poem extracts and answer the questions next to them.

Change

The spring
still comes
like a whisper in the dark night.

Charlotte Zolotow

● *What is the coming of spring compared to?*

● *Does this make you think of spring coming noisily or quietly?*

City Scene

See-saw sky-scraper,
pocked with holes like
a nutmeg grater.

Beverley Harry

● *What are the holes in the sky-scraper?*

● *What is suggested by the word pocked?*

● *In what ways are the sky-scraper and the grater similar?*

Metaphors

A *metaphor* is a little bit different from a simile. The poet does not *compare* something to something else but actually says that it *is* something else. Look at the following example:

The Moon

The moon was but a chin of gold
A night or two ago,
And now she turns her perfect face
Upon the world below.

Emily Dickinson

Think about the shape of a chin and then of the colour of gold. This is the image the poet uses to describe the new moon. She uses a familiar part of the face to describe the moon's shape and the word *gold* to show how it shines in the sky. The image is then developed so that when the moon is full the chin has become a woman's *perfect face*.

ACTIVITY 3

Now write your own poem about the sun and how it appears at different times of the day and the year. Think about the images you could use to show your reader what it looks like. Start your poem with The sun is a...

ACTIVITY 4

Read the following poems and try to answer the questions next to them.

The Bee

The bee is a merchant.
He trades among
flower planets.

Peter Kelso

- What does a merchant do?
- Think about a bee. In what ways does he trade *among flowers*?
- What does the word planets *suggest*?

The Wind

The wind is a dog
flattening all this tall grass
before lying down.

Kevin Hart

- What damage does the wind do?
- Explain this image in your own words.

Colour

Sometimes poets use *colour* in interesting ways to put across a particular idea. We tend to associate colours with certain things. Think of the colour white. What things are white? Snow? A clean page? A wedding dress? What else? White tends to be associated with innocence and purity.

Make a list of the feelings and things you associate with these colours:

- black
- red
- grey.

In the poem on page 59 the poet uses the *metaphor* of a grey thread to describe her life. The coloured beads represent all the things that have happened to her that have brought colour into her life. Read the poem carefully then work through the questions in Activity 5 below.

ACTIVITY 5

1 How does the poet feel about her life in the first verse of the poem?

2 What do the following coloured beads represent?

   blue gold purple green yellow red crimson silver white?

3 How does the poet feel about her life by the end of the poem?

4 What do you think of this image of a person's life being a grey thread with many different coloured beads on it? Is it interesting? Does it work well?

5 Think of the important things in your life. Make a list of them. What colour beads would you choose to represent each of them? Write the colours next to the items on your list and explain why you have chosen them.

The Grey Thread

My life is a grey thread,
A thin grey stretched out thread,
And when I trace its course, I moan:
How dull! How dead!

5   But I have gay beads.
A pale one to begin,
A blue one for my painted dreams,
And one for sin,
Gold with coiled marks,
10 Like a snake's skin.

For love an odd bead
With a deep purple glow;
A green bead for a secret thing
That few shall know;
15 And yellow for my thoughts
That melt like snow.

A red bead for my strength,
And crimson for my hate;
Silver for the songs I sing
20 When I am desolate;
And white for my laughter
That mocks trickster fate.

My life is a grey thread
Stretching through Time's day;
25 But I have slipped gay, gorgeous
     beads on it
To hide the grey.

Elsa Gidlow

Personification

Sometimes, to get a particular idea across to the reader, a poet will give a thing that is without life characteristics that suggest it is alive, like a person or an animal. This is known as *personification*. You have already seen this in the poem **The Moon** (page 57) where the moon is described as a woman with a perfect face. In the following poem it is the sun and the sky that are made to seem alive.

Sunday Morning

Sunday morning

       and the sun
       bawls
       with
5   his big mouth

Yachts

       paper triangles
       of white and blue
       crowd the sloping bay
10   appearing motionless
       as if stuck there
       by some infant thumb

       beneath a shouting sky

       upon a painted sea

Wes Magee

ACTIVITY 6

1 How is the sun described? What do the words *bawls* and *his big mouth* suggest?

2 Explain, without using the words of the poem, what you think the sun is like on this particular morning.

3 How is the sky described? What does this suggest to you?

4 Now look at the way the yachts in the sea are described. Notice how they are *motionless*, not moving at all. The sea looks as though it is a painting with no movement or life in it. This is almost the opposite of the images of the sun and the sky, which are very much alive. How do the last two lines of the poem emphasize this difference?

Dialect

Another feature of language in some poems is the use of *dialect*. This means that poets will write in the way that a particular person might speak. It helps the readers to understand the person better and to feel that they are being spoken to directly. In the poem opposite, **Unrelated Incidents**, the poet writes in the way a person from Glasgow might speak.

ACTIVITY 7

1 Make up your own short report on an item of recent news.

2 Rewrite it in a dialect of your choice. The spelling of the words should show how they are meant to be spoken.

from Unrelated Incidents

this is thi
six a clock
news thi
man said n
5 thi reason
a talk wia
BBC accent
iz coz yi
widny wahnt
10 mi ti talk
aboot thi
trooth wia
voice lik
wanna yoo
15 scruff. if
a toktaboot
thi trooth
lik wanna yoo
scruff yi
20 widny thingk
it wuz troo.
jist wanna yoo
scruff tokn.
thirza right
25 way ti spell
ana right way
ti tok it. this
is me tokn yir
right way a
30 spellin. this
is ma trooth.
yooz doant no
thi trooth
yirsellz cawz
35 yi canny talk
right. this is
the six a clock
nyooz. belt up.

Tom Leonard

Test yourself

Read the following poem, which is about a man who used to live on a Caribbean island but who now lives in London. The notes at the side of the poem will help you to understand the meaning better. Once you have read and understood the poem answer the questions that follow it.

Island Man

Morning
and island man wakes up
to the sound of blue surf
in his head
5 the steady breaking and wombing

wild seabirds
and fishermen pushing out to sea
the sun surfacing defiantly

from the east
10 of his small emerald island
he always comes back   groggily groggily

Comes back to sands
of a grey metallic soar
         to surge of wheels
15 to dull North Circular roar

muffling muffling
his crumpled pillow waves
island man heaves himself

Another London day

Grace Nichols

*as he wakes he
hears the sea of
his island home*

*in his mind he
sees the birds
and the fishermen*

he awakes slowly

*he hears the sound
of London traffic*

*his dream of his island
mixes with the reality
of life in London*

*his life in
London goes on*

1 What different colours are used in the poem?

2 What do the colours show you about the man's feelings for his island home and for London?

3 What does the poet say about the sun? What does this suggest?

4 Which words are repeated? What effect does this have?

5 It is usually birds that soar. What do the words *grey metallic soar* (line 13) suggest?

6 In what way is his pillow like the sea?

7 What do the words *heaves himself* suggest to you?

Choosing the right material

In exams you may be asked to write about more than one poem. You will have talked about and studied all the poems in class before the exam. So what you need to learn now is how to put what you know about the poems together in order to answer a specific question.

Read the poem on this page and the one on page 64 carefully. Try reading them aloud. Think about where you should pause and the tone of voice you should use. Do not answer the questions next to them yet.

In the first poem, **Incendiary**, the poet writes about a young boy who is so desperately in need of affection that he sets fire to a farm, causing a great deal of damage.

Incendiary

That one small boy with face like pallid cheese
And burnt-out little eyes could make a blaze
As brazen, fierce and huge, as red and gold
And zany yellow as the one that spoiled
5 Three thousand guineas' worth of property
And crops at Godwin's Farm on Saturday
Is frightening – as fact and metaphor:
An ordinary match intended for
The lighting of a pipe or kitchen fire
10 Misused may set a whole menagerie
Of flame-fanged tigers roaring hungrily.
And frightening, too, that one small boy should set
The sky on fire and choke the stars to heat
Such skinny limbs and such a little heart
15 Which would have been content with one warm kiss
Had there been anyone to offer this.

Vernon Scannell

What does brazen mean?

How much damage did the boy cause?

Fill in the missing word in this sentence. The poet finds it f_____ that the boy could do this.

What words are used to describe the flames?

What would the boy have been content with?

What colours are used to describe the blaze?

When did the boy do this?

What did the boy use to start the fire?

What does the word menagerie mean?

What time of day was it?

Why did the boy do it?

In the second poem, **Attention Seeking**, the poet adopts the voice of a young
boy who believes he is in need of attention.

Attention Seeking

I'm needing attention.
I know I'm needing attention
because I hear people say it.
People that know these things.
5 I'm needing attention,
so what I'll do is steal something.
I know I'll steal something
because that is what I do
when I'm needing attention.
10 Or else I'll mess up my sister's room,
throw all her clothes on to the floor,
put her gerbil under her pillow
and lay a trap above the door (terrible)
a big heavy dictionary to drop on her
15 when she comes through. (Swot.)
This is the kind of thing I do
when I'm needing attention.
But I'm never boring.
I always think up new things.
20 Attention has lots of colours
and tunes. And lots of punishments.
For attention you can get detention.
Extra homework. Extra housework.
All sorts of things. Although
25 yesterday I heard the woman say
that I was just needing
someone to listen. My dad went mad.
'Listen to him!' he said. 'Listen!
You've got to be joking.'
30 Mind you, that was right after
I stole his car keys and drove
his car straight into the wall.
I wasn't hurt, but I'm still
needing quite a lot of attention.

Jackie Kay

Who is the 'I' in the poem?

Who do you think these people are?

What does the boy do to get attention?

What do you think lines 20 and 21 mean?

How is the boy punished?

Who do you think this woman might be?

What does she suggest?

How does the father react to her suggestion?

Why is the father so angry?

Meaning

Once you have read the poems a number of times the next stage is to work out what they are about. Now answer the questions that appear alongside these poems. Once you have done this you should be able to put your ideas together to write accounts of both of them. Here is a sample summary of the poem, **Incendiary**:

> **Incendiary** by Vernon Scannell is about a small boy who sets fire to a farm one Saturday night. He causes a lot of damage to the property and crops at Godwin's farm. The boy used an ordinary match to start the fire which looks like 'flame-fanged tigers roaring hungrily'. The poet finds it frightening that the boy should start the fire. He seems to have done this because he had no one to love him or give him 'one warm kiss'.

ACTIVITY 1

Look back at your answers to the questions on **Incendiary** and **Attention Seeking** and use them to write an account of each poem.

Form

Now that you know what the poems are about you need to think about their *form*. What can you say about the way they are set out? Are they in verses or in a single block? Do they have a regular or irregular *rhythm*? Count the beats in each line to work out the answer.

Where do you need to pause, when reading the poems aloud, to make the meaning come across as clearly as possible?

What use do the poets make of *rhyme*? Can you find words that rhyme? Can you find words that don't quite rhyme but are very close in sound? Are there any examples of words that rhyme within a line?

Look for examples of *repetition* of words and phrases (groups of words) in both poems. Make a list of these. Why do you think the poets have chosen to repeat these particular words and phrases?

Language

Now you need to think about the words the poets use and the ways they use them.

ACTIVITY 2

Copy out the following passage, then fill in the missing words from the box below.

Attention Seeking is written as though it were the _____ speaking directly to the reader. This lets the _____ see things through the boy's eyes. The boy uses slang phrases such as _____. The sentences are quite short and the language is fairly _____ and straightforward. The word S*wot* has two meanings. It could mean that the _____ is someone who works hard or it could be referring to the heavy _____ hitting her as she walks through the door. Attention is described as having _____. This suggests that there are lots of different, interesting ways of getting attention.

sister	boy	dictionary	*lots of colours. / And tunes.*
simple	reader	*My dad went mad*	

ACTIVITY 3

Read the poem **Incendiary** again, then answer these questions.

1 What do the words *pallid cheese* and *burnt-out little eyes* suggest about the appearance of the boy in **Incendiary**?

2 The fire is described as *a whole menagerie / Of flame-fanged tigers roaring hungrily*. Explain why this is a good description of a fire.

3 How do the words *skinny limbs* and *such a little heart* help to make the reader feel sorry for the boy?

Personal response

Before you are able to compare these two poems you need to decide what you think about each of them.

In what ways are they similar and different? Think about their meaning and the way they are written.

What do you think the two boys are like? Why do you think this? Which boy do you feel most sympathy for? Why?

What do you like or dislike about the ways the poets have used language? Can you give particular examples?

Which poem do you like most? Give at least three reasons for your choice.

Test *yourself*

1 Imagine you are the boy in **Incendiary**. Explain what happened on the night you set fire to Godwin's Farm. Try to give your reasons for doing this.

2 Imagine you are the Dad in **Attention Seeking**. Write about your son. Say what he is like and why you think he behaves as he does.

3 Read through all the work you have done on these two poems. Write a paragraph on each of the following:

- what the poems are about

- the way the words have been set out on the page

- the way words are used

- what you think about the poems.

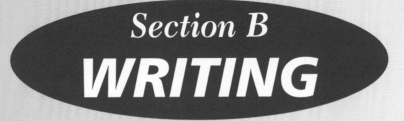

Section B
WRITING

Writing

There are lots of different types of writing. People write diaries, letters, notes, stories, poems, newspaper articles, leaflets and many other things. Anything that is written has a purpose and an audience – a reason for being written and an intended reader.

Different kinds of writing require different skills and different levels of effort. A note written to a friend is written quickly, doesn't need much planning and is generally informal. A letter to a would-be employer, on the other hand, needs a lot of thought, careful planning and is written in standard English.

It is important that you learn to match your writing to the standards expected of it. When making notes, for example, you can waste a lot of time by writing in complete sentences. Similarly, if you're asked to explain something factual and you end up writing a story instead, then you are wasting your readers' time. You need to be clear on what you are being asked to do and how to do it.

This section will help you to improve your *writing skills*. You will find:

- examples of the different kinds of writing you will be asked to do in GCSE English

- advice on how to write in particular ways

- help on how to plan, sequence and develop your own ideas.

Writing to instruct, persuade or argue are tested in NEAB GCSE English, Paper 1 Section B.

Writing to inform, explain or describe are tested in NEAB GCSE English, Paper 2 Section B.

Writing to instruct

When *writing to instruct* your aim is to tell your reader how to do something. In our everyday life, we are surrounded by writing that instructs us in one way or another.

A ▼

ACTIVITY 1

Read texts A, B and C. For each one, write down:

● what kind of text it is

● where you would be most likely to find it.

Now make your own list of examples of **writing to instruct**. You could start by looking around your classroom or thinking about things in your home.

Toners

WELLA

**WASH IN - WASH OUT
FOR NOTICEABLE COLOUR & SHINE**

675-NUTMEG

A rich warm brown to enliven mousey hair.

Instructions for use
Wet hair, lather in Toners. Leave for 5 minutes. **Lasts about 3 washes** depending on hair condition. For a more noticeable result, leave for up to 20 minutes. Rinse clear.

For a longer lasting colour result try Wella Colour Mousse.

C ▼

INSERTION & REMOVAL OF CASSETTE TAPE

The cassette tape should be inserted into the unit with the cassette tape opening, facing upwards towards the buttons.

Close the cassette door before PLAYBACK.

Before attempting to remove the cassette, ensure that the STOP button has been pressed and then open the cassette door.

PLAYBACK

Open the cassette door by hand and insert the cassette tape.

Push the cassette door lightly to close it.

Press the PLAY button.

Adjust the volume to a comfortable, safe listening level.

Stop the cassette tape by pushing the STOP button.

FAST FORWARD

To advance the tape rapidly, press FAST FORWARD then press the STOP button before pressing PLAY.

B ▼

BANANA FROTHIES

Serves 4

INGREDIENTS

2 bananas
300 ml (½ pint) cold milk
300 ml (½ pint) plain yoghurt
2 tablespoons clear honey

YOU WILL NEED

knife
chopping board
measuring jug
tablespoon
blender goblet
4 medium glasses
4 straws

Preparation time: 10 minutes

1 Peel and slice the bananas and put them in the blender goblet. Add the milk, yoghurt and honey. Blend for 30–40 seconds until you have a smooth, frothy liquid. (Ask an adult to help you do this.)

2 Pour the frothy drink into 4 medium glasses and serve at once with straws.

Features of writing to instruct

There are certain features that are often found in this kind of writing.

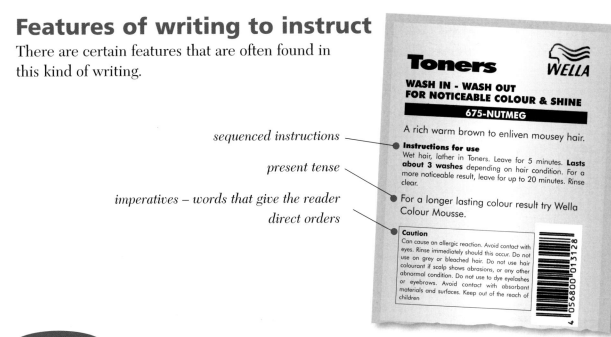

sequenced instructions

present tense

imperatives – words that give the reader direct orders

Toners *WELLA*

WASH IN - WASH OUT
FOR NOTICEABLE COLOUR & SHINE
675-NUTMEG

A rich warm brown to enliven mousey hair.

● **Instructions for use**
Wet hair, lather in Toners. Leave for 5 minutes. **Lasts about 3 washes** depending on hair condition. For a more noticeable result, leave for up to 20 minutes. Rinse clear.

● For a longer lasting colour result try Wella Colour Mousse.

● **Caution**
Can cause an allergic reaction. Avoid contact with eyes. Rinse immediately should this occur. Do not use on grey or bleached hair. Do not use hair colourant if scalp shows abrasions, or any other abnormal condition. Do not use to dye eyelashes or eyebrows. Avoid contact with absorbant materials and surfaces. Keep out of the reach of children

ACTIVITY 2

1 The following simple sentences are written in the **past** tense. Rewrite them, using the **present** tense. The first one has been done for you.

  ● He walked to school.

    He walks to school

  ● He found a piece of paper.

  ● He picked it up and looked at it.

  ● The date on the paper was April 1st, 1904.

2 Put the following sentences in the correct **sequence** or order.

  a She opened her eyes.

  b She got out of bed.

  c She went downstairs.

  d She made some tea and toast.

  e The alarm clock rang.

  f She got dressed.

3 Write out the instructions opposite for how to make a cup of tea. Underline the **imperatives** in them. Remember, imperatives are words that give the reader direct orders.

Put water in the kettle and boil it. Take a cup off the stand and place a tea bag in it. When the kettle has boiled fill the cup with boiling water. Leave for a few moments and then remove the tea bag from the cup. Finally add milk and/or sugar according to taste.

4 Now write your own **instructions** for two of the following:

  ● how to get from your house to your school

  ● how to clean your teeth

  ● how to make beans on toast.

Try to follow these steps carefully:

  ● list the details you need to include

  ● place them in the correct sequence – it may help to number them

  ● write in the present tense

  ● use imperatives.

Audience and purpose

When writing, a writer usually has a particular audience and purpose in mind. The audience of a piece of writing is the intended reader, the person (or people) it is written for.

The purpose of a piece of writing is the reason for which it has been written.

ACTIVITY 3

Draw a table with three columns, like the one below. Label the columns **Text**, **Audience** and **Purpose**. Try to identify the audience and purpose of each of the three texts on page 72. The first one is done for you:

TEXT	AUDIENCE	PURPOSE
Text A	Someone who wants to lightly colour their hair – probably female	To instruct them how to use the colourant properly

Leaflets and advice sheets

Many *leaflets* and *advice sheets* contain writing to instruct. Sometimes the instructions are grouped together under sub-headings. The instructions are always directly targeted at the audience and purpose. Read the following *leaflet:*

Don't lose your VOTE

Why should I vote?

This country is a democracy. Every day, vital decisions affecting all our lives are taken by Members of Parliament and local councillors elected by the people. You can help choose them. Make sure you have your say – use your right to vote. If you don't, you will lose your chance to influence the way things are run in the country, or your part of it. All votes are equal – your vote is as important as anyone else's.

Can anyone vote?

No. You have to be 18 or over. You must also be:

✗ a British citizen; or
✗ a citizen of another Commonwealth country; or
✗ a citizen of the Republic of Ireland; or
✗ for certain elections, a citizen of another European Union country.

Your name must be included on the register of electors, otherwise you can't vote.

How do I get on the register?

That's easy. Each year, at the end of the summer, the local Electoral Registration Officer (whose job is to compile the register) sends the electoral registration form (called Form A) to every household in his or her area.

If your household has not received the form by the middle of September contact the Electoral Registration Officer at your local council offices. Form A has to be filled in by one of the householders.

If you are a citizen of another European Union country, ask the Electoral Registration Officer for an application form.

✗ If you live in a hostel the form should be filled in by the people who run it.

✗ If you are a lodger in someone's house it should be filled in by the owner of the house.

✗ If you live in a flat with friends, one person should take responsibility for filling in the form.

✗ If you live on your own, in a bedsit for example, you should fill in the form.

HOME OFFICE
PUBLICATIONS

ACTIVITY 4

1 What audience is the leaflet on page 74 written for? Is it:

- adults who already have a vote
- 18-year-olds who are now old enough to vote
- 16–17-year-olds who will soon be able to vote
- adults who no longer wish to use their vote?

2 What is the purpose of the leaflet? Is it:

- to make young people vote
- to encourage young people to register for voting?

3 What tense is used in the leaflet? Is it:

- past
- present
- future?

4 What sub-headings are used to help organize the information?

Read the *advice sheets* on this page, which are both about drugs. They have different audiences and purposes.

A ▼

How to help a friend who has a problem with drugs

We all need friends. Sometimes we need the help they can give us. Sometimes it is our turn to help them out. If someone you know has a problem with drugs...

- STICK BY THEM. DON'T TURN YOUR BACK ON THEM.
- LISTEN TO THEM AND HOW THEY SAY THEY FEEL.
- DON'T START SLAGGING THEM OFF TO THEIR FACE OR TO OTHER PEOPLE.
- SUGGEST WHAT THEY MIGHT DO BUT DON'T KEEP ON ABOUT IT. THEY WILL HAVE TO MAKE THEIR OWN DECISIONS.
- IF THEY WANT, OFFER TO GO WITH THEM IF THEY ARE GOING TO SEEK HELP FROM A DRUG AGENCY, DOCTOR, COUNSELLOR OR WHOEVER.
- ENCOURAGE THEM TO BE POSITIVE ABOUT THEMSELVES.
- ENCOURAGE THEM TO FEEL THEY CAN DO SOMETHING POSITIVE ABOUT THEIR PROBLEMS.

It can be hard work helping someone who has a problem with drugs. Then again it's not much fun for them and anyway what are mates for?

HEALTH EDUCATION AUTHORITY

B ▼

WHAT TO DO IN AN EMERGENCY

It is vitally important that you know what to do should the worst happen and you find your child drowsy or unconscious. It could save their life. Whatever you do, don't panic.

First make sure they've got plenty of fresh air.

Then turn them on to their side. Try not to leave them alone because if they are sick, they could inhale vomit.

Dial 999 and ask for an ambulance.

Collect up anything that seems to have been used in the drug taking – tablets, powders, solvents etc. – and give them to a member of the ambulance crew.

ACTIVITY 5

1 Identify the audience and purpose in Text A.

2 Identify the audience and purpose in Text B.

3 List the words and phrases in each text which help you to identify the audience and purpose.

Writing to instruct needn't always be so serious. Sometimes it can be fun.
Read the extract below, which gives some tips on how to have a good New Year.

Sugary resolutions

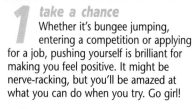

A WHOLE YEAR AHEAD
AND SO MUCH TO FIT
IN. WHATEVER YOU DO,
SQUEEZE THESE INTO
YOUR SCHEDULE AND
YOU'LL GUARANTEE THAT
THIS YEAR IS A GOOD-UN!

10 things you just gotta do this year!

1 take a chance
Whether it's bungee jumping, entering a competition or applying for a job, pushing yourself is brilliant for making you feel positive. It might be nerve-racking, but you'll be amazed at what you can do when you try. Go girl!

2 say no
Whether it's doing your mates' homework or getting steamy with your boy – summon up some sassiness and say no. Get some respect y'all!

3 throw a party
OK it with your folks, choose a theme – an Easter Egg bash or apple-bobbing affair for Halloween – then get your friends together for a jolly good knees-up. It'll be a blast to organize and you'll be known henceforth as *the* Party Princess.

4 list your life
Write down the 10 things you want most out of your life this year, then go out and get 'em. Keep your list somewhere safe and tick 'em off as you go. Jan 1 is day one, so get cracking!

5 fall in love
It could be luscious Leonardo or the lifeguard at your local pool, but that stomach churning, toe tingling, head full of bubbles lurve feeling is the best. And you know what? It makes your skin glow too!

6 value your bezzies
Grab hold of your best buds, stock up on tons of munchies – like banana milkshake and cookies – whack on summat corny like *Mary Poppins*, *Grease* or *The Sound of Music*, and sing the blimmin' house down. There's nowt like it for clearing out the cobwebs.

7 give something up
Got a really annoying habit that you know you'd be so much better off without? Whether it's biting your nails, saying 'innit?' or wearing your socks two days in a row, now's the time to nip that niggle in the bud and sort out your life!

8 join a charidee
Don't just sit around ranting and raving about life's injustices – *do* something! Whether it's preserving the turtle population, fighting racism or joining Amnesty International, if it matters to you, you'll feel a whole lot better if you start doing something about it!

9 clear out your clobber
From those scary spangly leggings, to the 'friend' who always puts you down, this is *the* year to sort your stuff and make your life totally klutz-free. And don't put it off 'til next December either!

10 kiss and make-up
OK, so you and a certain someone had a bit of a fall-out and now you're not speaking – but does it *really* matter? Life's too short to bear grudges, so why not start over for the new year? Destiny will smile upon you for all eternity. Or something.

SUGAR MAGAZINE

ACTIVITY 6

1 The language in this text is informal and has been chosen specifically to suit a teenage audience, for example:

● *Go girl!*

● *summon up some sassiness*

● *Get some respect y'all!*

Find as many other examples as you can.

2 These 'resolutions' or instructions are written for teenage girls. Make up four instructions that would be suitable for teenage boys. Try to make your language appropriate to your audience.

Test *yourself*

Write a leaflet instructing your teachers on how to make school a better place for the pupils.

Start by following these stages, step by step.

1 Identify the audience and the purpose.

2 Gather ideas. Think about:

- uniform ● school rules
- assemblies ● length of lessons
- subjects studied ● punishments
- rewards ● careers advice
- options ● class groupings
- different ways of teaching.

Write a list of the points you want to make about each idea.

Are there other things you want to write about?

3 Decide on the best order for your instructions. Number them. At this stage you may decide to leave some of your original ideas out.

4 Think of possible sub-headings, e.g. points on length of lessons, subjects studied and different ways of teaching could be grouped together under the sub-heading 'Lessons'.

5 Here is an example of how you could start your writing, using a leaflet style and a question and answer approach:

How you could make school a better place

We all want school to be as good as it can be. Here's how you, the teachers, could help to make it better for us, the pupils.

Changing the rules

Is it really necessary for pupils to wear uniform? Make pupils happier by letting them wear their own clothes to school. Allow them to be individuals.

Why should pupils have to line up outside the classrooms? Let them go in and sit down as soon as they arrive. Give them the chance to get comfortable before the lesson begins.

Do you have to call the register every lesson? Look around the classroom and simply tick off the names of pupils who are present.

Now write your own instructions under the following sub-headings:

- Getting the lessons right
- Rewards and punishments
- Careers advice.

Remember also to:

- sequence your points
- state your points clearly
- write in the present tense
- use imperatives
- use language that is appropriate to your audience.

6 Once you have written your instructions check through them again carefully. Are they direct? Are they clear? Are they appropriate to your purpose and audience?

Writing to persuade

When you are *writing to persuade* your aim is to make your reader do something or believe something.

The following charity letter hopes to persuade its readers that people on the streets desperately need their help. Read the letter below carefully.

Will the next person you see sleeping rough still be alive in the morning?

Dear Reader,

Make no mistake, life on the streets really does kill. I have seen it time after time. Recently Shelter workers found a man sleeping rough who had frostbite. He died before they got him to hospital. Nobody knew his name.

Think of it. Dying cold, hungry and alone.

This cruel vision – homeless people lying dead on the streets from the cold – is why Shelter has launched its Winter Nights appeal.

Our aim is to help set up a network of emergency overnight accommodation across the country in schools, churches and hospitals during those bleak, freezing months.

We want to ensure that cold and hungry people, wherever they are, can find a bed for the night.

So I'm writing to ask you if you can make a gift. Something which will help stop homeless people dying on our streets this winter.

The cold and the rain take a harsh toll on bodies already weakened by poor nutrition. <u>All over the country homeless people are in desperate need of warmth, food and shelter.</u>

Our aim is to make thousands of bed spaces available nationwide during the harshest weather. Can you help Shelter meet the need?

Your gift to the Winter Nights' appeal could help save lives.

I still remember John. I was fond of John. He was what they call 'a bit of a character'.

We were talking one day about his health, and the coming winter. He said in a curiously matter-of-fact way, 'Of course, it's going to kill me'.

A few months later, one freezing morning, they found his body in the rough shelter which he'd made.

John wasn't just another statistic. He was a human being, and he deserved better.

Nobody chooses to sleep rough in the wet and the cold. Nobody wants to be homeless.

Without the Winter Nights' appeal, more homeless people risk death in the coming months.

Worse still, there's a new and worrying development. <u>And that's the number of children – youngsters under 16 – who are now sleeping on the streets</u>. Often these youngsters have been in Local Authority care. They haven't had a family's help and support to start with. They've grown up in institutions, and now they're trying to make their way in the world alone.

It's an outrage to leave vulnerable kids like these out on the streets, a prey to the cruelty of the winter weather and to every unsavoury character who offers them 'help'.

Changes are desperately needed.

Your help is desperately needed.

January and February bring the coldest nights of the year. And that means <u>homeless people on the streets will die</u> unless they get the kind of help that the Winter Nights' appeal will provide.

They <u>need</u> our help. Please make an effort to give something to the Winter Nights' appeal. When you do, you will be helping freezing cold, homeless people survive the coldest nights of the year.

Tony Harvey

Outreach worker

SHELTER LETTER

Devices

The writer uses a number of devices which are common to *writing to persuade*.

Rhetorical questions

These are questions that are designed to involve the reader. They make you think.

Before the main part of the letter the reader is asked:

Will the next person you see sleeping rough still be alive in the morning?

This makes you think about the people on the streets and their chances of surviving the night.

Personal evidence

This makes you more aware of the writer and makes the situation seem more real. The Shelter letter starts with the story of a man with frostbite who died before he could be got to hospital. It is made more sad by the fact that nobody knew his name.

ACTIVITY 1

1 Find one other **rhetorical question** in the letter. Explain what it makes the reader think about.

2 Find another example of personal evidence in the letter. Explain how it makes the problem seem more real.

Bold print and underlining

These features are used to emphasize a particular point and to draw the reader's attention to it.

ACTIVITY 2

Bold print is used four times in the letter. Read those bits again.

● What are they about?

● What does the writer hope to emphasize?

Make a list of the words that are <u>underlined</u> in the letter. Explain why the writer has underlined these words.

Repetition

Sometimes words are repeated to make sure the reader has got the message, for example:

● *Changes are desperately needed.*

● *Your help is desperately needed.*

At other times it is the ideas that are repeated.

ACTIVITY 3

● How many times does the idea of people dying on the streets appear in the letter?

● Why does the writer do this?

Emotive language

The most important feature of writing to persuade is the way the writer uses words to appeal to the feelings of the reader. This is known as *emotive* use of language.

Look at the following:

> Think of it. Dying cold, hungry and alone.
> This cruel vision – homeless people lying dead on the streets from the cold ...

The words are simple and to the point. They invite the reader to imagine what it must be like to die in this way. The build-up of words *cold, hungry and alone* creates a picture in the mind of the reader. The word *cruel* emphasizes how awful this is and this is reinforced by the idea of the *homeless people lying dead on the streets from the cold.*

ACTIVITY 4

Look at these short extracts from the letter, then answer the questions on them.

1 *Nobody knew his name.*

- What does this detail tell you about the man who died?

2 *those bleak, freezing months.*

- What does the word *bleak* mean? Why do you think the writer chose to use this word?

3 *John wasn't just another statistic. He was a human being, and he deserved better.*

- What does the writer mean by saying that John wasn't just a statistic? What point is he trying to bring home to the reader?

4 *It's an <u>outrage</u> to leave <u>vulnerable</u> kids like these out on the streets, a <u>prey</u> to the <u>cruelty</u> of the winter weather and to every <u>unsavoury</u> character who offers them 'help'.*

- What do the underlined words mean?
- What do they add to the overall effect of the sentence?
- Why is the word *help* placed in inverted commas?

ACTIVITY 5

Read the account of Janice below.

Using the information given here and your own ideas, write a short appeal to readers of a teenage magazine, asking them to help youngsters like Janice. Start your appeal with the question 'Can You Help Janice?'

A quarter of people living rough are aged 25 or under

Janice

Her parents broke up when she was ten. Her mum's new boyfriend began to beat her. And at fourteen, when his sexual abuse wouldn't stop, she ran away.

Janice has spent a third of her life living rough. She's been beaten up in back alleys and sexually assaulted so often she doesn't even want to talk about it. Sitting in shop doorways, all Janice can think about is how much she wants to die.

SHELTER/CRISIS WINTERWATCH SURVEY

Test *yourself*

Write a letter to the Governors of your school. Your aim is to persuade them to donate the profits from a school concert to the charity of your choice. Follow these stages.

1 First of all, decide on the charity. Choose one that you know something about. You can, if you like, choose Shelter.

2 List the reasons why your chosen charity is worth supporting.

3 List examples of the work your charity does. These can be made up.

4 Decide how you are going to organize your material. Perhaps you can match reasons to examples. It may help to number the points in the order in which you are going to write them.

5 Make notes on the ways you could use:

   - **rhetorical questions** to make your readers think

   - **personal evidence** to support the points you make

   - **repetition** to give your words more effect

   - **emotive language** to touch the feelings of your readers.

6 When writing a **formal letter** there are certain things you need to do. Set your letter out like the example below:

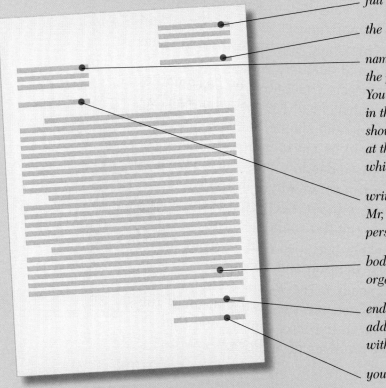

full address and postcode

the day's date in full

name (if known), title and address of the person to whom you are writing. You do not have to use punctuation in the addresses, but if you do you should be consistent, placing a comma at the end of each line until the last which should end with a full stop

write Dear Sir, Dear Madam or Dear Mr, Ms, Miss or Mrs, followed by the person's last name (surname)

body of your letter with ideas organized into paragraphs

end with Yours sincerely, if you have addressed the recipient by name and with Yours faithfully, if you have not

your signature

7 When you have finished writing, check through your work carefully. Are your ideas expressed clearly? Do you want to add anything or take anything out? Are there any bits you want to make **bold** or <u>underline</u> for emphasis? Finally, don't forget to sign your letter!

Writing to argue

When *writing to argue* your aim is to present and develop a particular point of view.

Opinion

Letters to newspapers and magazines often present an argument. This is usually based on the writer's opinion. Read the following letters carefully, then do the tasks and answer the questions in Activities 1 and 2.

A ▶

We need something really special to celebrate worldwide the start of the 21st century. Not some fantasy dome or decorated mugs to give to schoolchildren. What we need is something that would improve the living standards of the under-privileged people in this very unequal world.

We should challenge the architects who designed the Millennium Dome to design the world's cheapest houses and help Third World countries turn their shanty towns and slums into clean and healthy dwelling places.

The architects could start by designing a modern equivalent of the forties prefabs – factory made and simple to erect. Today's prefabs could be cheaply produced on automated production lines and transported in containers to anywhere in the world.

In areas without electricity, small solar panels on the flat roofs linked to rechargeable batteries could provide enough power for lighting and a radio.

All it needs is the will of the rich countries and the co-operation of the rest to make the next century one that changes the lives of millions.

D. STREETER, BRIGHTON

Why in this day and age do we still have uniforms in schools? No one I know likes wearing their uniform. Pupils would be much happier if they could wear their own clothes to school and there would be far fewer silly arguments over why you haven't got a tie on or how many earrings you can wear. Just think of the time the teachers could save if they didn't have to check uniform.

It's not just that, though. Clothes are a way of expressing individuality. I choose my clothes to say something about the kind of person I am. Individuality is a good thing. We don't all want to grow up like sheep just following the leader, do we? So why should we all have to wear the same clothes?

It's not even as though we get to choose what the uniform should be. My school has had the same uniform ever since my oldest sister was here and she left ten years ago!

I've just finished school and finally I can throw my hated uniform in the bin, at least most of it. There's one thing I intend to keep and that's the shirt I wore on the last day. It's covered in my friends' names and I shall keep it always – the only bit of my uniform I've ever taken pride in!

Karen, Nottingham

B

The key points of the argument in letter A are that:

- we need something special with which to celebrate the 21st century
- architects should be challenged to design cheap houses
- this would help Third World countries
- solar panels could be used in areas without electricity
- this can be achieved with the will of the rich countries and the co-operation of the rest.

As well as presenting an argument in favour of building cheap houses for Third World countries the letter attacks what is currently being done to celebrate the millennium.

ACTIVITY 1

1 List the key points in letter B.

2 Does letter B contain any facts?

3 Does letter B contain any opinions that are stated as facts?

4 What use does Karen from Nottingham make of questions and exclamations? What effect do these have?

ACTIVITY 2

Make a list of key points that could be included in a letter in favour of school uniform.

Fact and opinion

The arguments in the letters on pages 84 and 85 are based on personal opinions. Sometimes writers use both *facts* and *opinions* when developing an argument, as in the article below.

Problems of Alcohol

Is the government as serious about tackling crime as it claims?

Statistics show:

1. 80–90% of all murders are committed by people who are under the influence of alcohol.

2. 60% of burglaries are carried out, according to police, by people under the influence of alcohol.

3. 70% (approx.) of child abuse, domestic violence and general anti-social behaviour is committed by people under the influence of alcohol.

4. BMA statistics reveal at least 40,000 people die each year as a direct result of alcohol consumption (compared to 300 or so from illegal drugs).

If one is serious about tackling crime would it not be obvious to tackle the alcohol issue? Education and awareness are badly needed to focus on what drinking alcohol can lead to; that alcohol can be a deadly drug in more ways than one; that it can be very addictive and should be treated with the greatest care. Drinking large quantities of alcohol affects the mind in many ways and this must be brought home to people, especially the young.

This Government is clearly neglecting its duty to educate and inform the public of the perils of alcohol binges and addiction. Could it be that the Government is only concerned about protecting the vast profits made out of selling booze?

Why is the sole thrust of Government and media power directed at what the authorities have deemed to be illegal? 'The Illegal Drugs Menace' is a tea party compared to the effects alcohol has on society.

MS DELIA O'HENNESSY

THE BIG ISSUE

SOURCED FROM *ESSENTIAL ARTICLES IV,*
THE RESOURCE FILE FOR ISSUES, CAREL PRESS

ACTIVITY 3

1 What message does the writer hope to get across by quoting the four statistics placed at the start of the article?

2 Reread the first paragraph. Why, according to the writer, are education and awareness badly needed?

3 What question is asked in the second paragraph? What does this suggest?

4 The article is mainly about the dangers of alcohol. What new ideas are introduced in the final paragraph?

Argument and persuasion

Often a writer is trying to persuade a reader to his or her point of view by presenting a strong argument. In the following article the first two key points of the argument are underlined.

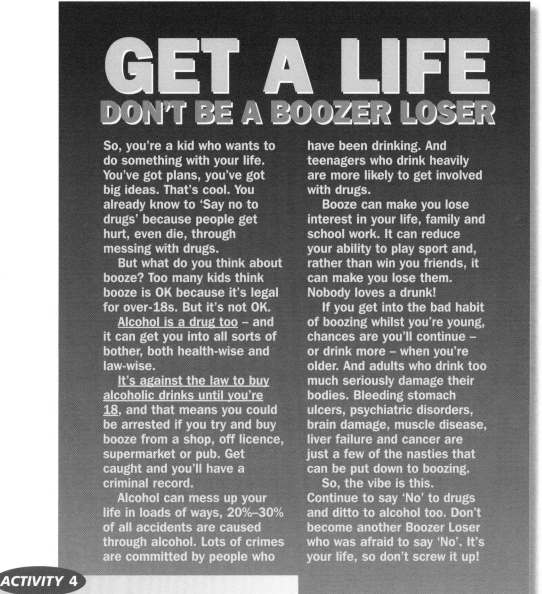

GET A LIFE
DON'T BE A BOOZER LOSER

So, you're a kid who wants to do something with your life. You've got plans, you've got big ideas. That's cool. You already know to 'Say no to drugs' because people get hurt, even die, through messing with drugs.

But what do you think about booze? Too many kids think booze is OK because it's legal for over-18s. But it's not OK. <u>Alcohol is a drug too</u> – and it can get you into all sorts of bother, both health-wise and law-wise.

<u>It's against the law to buy alcoholic drinks until you're 18</u>, and that means you could be arrested if you try and buy booze from a shop, off licence, supermarket or pub. Get caught and you'll have a criminal record.

Alcohol can mess up your life in loads of ways, 20%–30% of all accidents are caused through alcohol. Lots of crimes are committed by people who have been drinking. And teenagers who drink heavily are more likely to get involved with drugs.

Booze can make you lose interest in your life, family and school work. It can reduce your ability to play sport and, rather than win you friends, it can make you lose them. Nobody loves a drunk!

If you get into the bad habit of boozing whilst you're young, chances are you'll continue – or drink more – when you're older. And adults who drink too much seriously damage their bodies. Bleeding stomach ulcers, psychiatric disorders, brain damage, muscle disease, liver failure and cancer are just a few of the nasties that can be put down to boozing.

So, the vibe is this. Continue to say 'No' to drugs and ditto to alcohol too. Don't become another Boozer Loser who was afraid to say 'No'. It's your life, so don't screw it up!

QUEST MAGAZINE

ACTIVITY 4

1 List the other key points of the argument.

2 Identify the audience for this article.

3 List words and phrases that helped you to identify the audience.

4 Identify the purpose of this article.

5 Do you think the article will achieve its purpose? Give reasons for your answer.

Test yourself

Your local newspaper is running a competition looking for the best and most original articles on 'How we should improve our area'.

Write an article putting forward your argument. Follow the stages outlined below.

1   The audience for your article are the readers of your local newspaper. The purpose is to argue in favour of a particular idea or ideas.

First you need the idea(s). Here are some possibilities to think about:

- better sports/leisure facilities

- improving transport

- knocking down a derelict area and replacing it with a park

- tackling specific problems such as drug abuse or litter.

Write down how you think your area could be improved.

2   Make a list of the key points you want to make about:

- why your area needs this

- the difference it would make to your area.

3   Think of the arguments people might put up against your suggestion:

- 'what about the cost?'

- 'it's not practical'

- 'only a few would benefit'.

List the possible objections and how you could answer them.

4   What facts could you include to support your argument? Make a list of them.

5   Once you have gathered your ideas, you need to sequence them.

Here is a possible order for you to work to:

a   what your area needs and the reasons why

b   how this could be achieved

c   the objections people might make and your answers to these

d   the advantages your idea(s) would bring to the area

Label the different bits of your notes **a**, **b**, **c** or **d** depending on whereabouts in your article you want to put them.

6   You are now ready to start writing your article. First, decide on an eye-catching headline. Remember that the use of questions and exclamations can help to keep your readers' interest.

7   When you have finished writing, check through your work carefully. Have you covered all your key points? Is your argument clear? Is it likely to convince your readers? Do you want to add anything or take anything out?

Writing to inform

When you are *writing to inform* your aim is to tell your reader about something or someone.

Facts and opinions

Informative writing often contains *facts* and *opinions*. In this extract from his diary, Captain Scott recounts the death of one of his companions, Titus Oates.

Friday, 16 March or Saturday, 17. Lost track of dates, but think the last date is correct. Tragedy all along the line. At lunch, the day before yesterday, poor Titus Oates said he couldn't go on; he proposed we should leave him in his sleeping bag. That we could not do, and induced him to come on, on the afternoon march. In spite of its awful nature for him he struggled on and we made a few miles. At night he was worse and we knew the end had come.

Should this be found I want these facts recorded. Oates' last thoughts were of his Mother, but immediately before he took pride in thinking that his regiment would be pleased with the bold way in which he met his death. We can testify to his bravery. He has borne intense suffering for weeks without complaint, and to the very last was able and willing to discuss outside subjects. He did not – would not – give up hope to the very end. He was a brave soul. This was the end. He slept through the night before last, hoping not to wake; but he woke in the morning – yesterday. It was blowing a blizzard. He said 'I am going outside and may be some time.' He went out into the blizzard and we have not seen him since.

'CAPTAIN SCOTT'S DIARY' BY ROBERT FALCON SCOTT

On 18 January 1912, Captain Scott and his companions reached the South Pole in Antarctica. They never returned. On 17 November searchers found the tent with their frozen bodies – and Scott's last diary.

In this diary extract Scott writes mainly *facts*. He tells the reader what Oates did. The first fact is: the day before he died Oates said he couldn't go on. What other facts are given about what Oates did?

The extract also contains some *opinions*:

● *Tragedy all along the line.*　　● *He was a brave soul.*

ACTIVITY 1

Think about someone you admire and the things you would want to write about him or her. Make a list of the **facts** you would want to include. Make a separate list of the **opinions** you would want to include.

Other people's opinions

Often newspaper and magazine articles contain writing that informs. Read the following article about army courses for young people:

Messing about on early manoeuvres

It's pouring with rain. A wet soldier is guarding a collection of armoured cars inside a small barbed-wire compound. Beyond the wire is a small town with shops, schools, pubs and some down-at-heel housing estates. Bosnia? Ulster? No, this is Catterick, the North Yorkshire base of the British Army and temporary home to a group of teenage boys who have come to 'look at life' in the Army.

The Army has been running Look at Life courses for some years, and several thousand young people participate each year in the North Yorkshire area alone. 'We get the full ability range,' says Major Tony Ross, Army careers adviser for an area which covers 161 schools.

Pupils can be from Year 10 upwards and the Army claims that there is no discrimination. Girls are welcome, but a shortage of female instructors means that some residential courses are limited to boys. Budding squaddies have to be fit enough to cope with 'an active five days' and resilient enough to mix successfully with the other course participants, who could be

from several different schools and a range of ages.

'First of all they'll make a bed,' says Major Ross 'Then they'll realize that six o'clock comes twice in a day. They sit and eat meals with

soldiers, they'll go out on a night exercise. They'll see that sometimes it can get quite frightening – but it's got to be fun.'

Nick Hawgate is in Year 10 at the non-selective Tadcaster Grammar School. He has come on the course 'to see how the Army works, see how they train'.

Partner Andrew Kay has looked forward to the challenge of doing something different. Nick has never slept outside before, especially not in November in the pouring rain.

'I'm a bit worried about the weather,' he says with feeling.

The Army is not bothered about the weather, having full confidence in the kit the group is going to use.

'Full waterproofs, Goretex sleeping bags, night shelters,' says liaison officer Captain Alison Savage, and, she adds, 'The NCOs will be with them.'

Teachers who have sent their students on Look at Life courses are positive about the results. 'I don't have any anxieties,' says Mr Flood, the careers master at Tadcaster school. 'The boys think that they are a lot of fun, very challenging.'

TIMES EDUCATIONAL
SUPPLEMENT

ACTIVITY 2

In this article the writer quotes the words of Tony Ross, Nick Hawgate, Andrew Kay, Alison Savage and Mr Flood. Make a table with three columns as shown below. Write down who these people are and what they have said. The first one is done for you:

NAME	WHO THEY ARE	WHAT THEY SAY
Tony Ross	Major in the army	'We get the full ability range.' 'First of all they'll make a bed. Then they'll realize that six o'clock comes twice in a day. They sit and eat meals with soldiers, they'll go out on a night exercise. They'll see that sometimes it can get quite frightening – but it's got to be fun.'

By giving the ideas and opinions of a number of different people from various backgrounds the writer is able to give a fuller picture of what the Look at Life course is like.

ACTIVITY 3

Suppose you were asked to write informatively about a school visit to a theme park. What might the following people say? Invent names for them and write down two or three things that they might say. Aim to give a fuller picture of the theme park through their words.

- student
- coach driver
- theme park attendant
- theme park owner.
- teacher

Personal details

Many people write about their experiences while travelling. They tell their readers about the journeys they have made, the places they have been to and their impressions of these places.

In the following extract Smita Patel, a second-generation Indian, recalls her arrival at the city of Delhi with her boyfriend:

I remember arriving at Delhi airport at 3 a.m., feeling apprehensive and excited. I was really no more knowledgeable about what to expect than any other Western traveller. It was now 6 a.m. and though the sun had barely risen we were shocked by the sheer volume of people. The whole area outside the airport was packed with families, beggars, police, rickshaw wallahs, fruit vendors, taxi men, and of course the famed hotel sellers, relentlessly directing us to the 'best room in town'. Luckily we had met an American woman on the plane who was being met by her brother and despite being heavily jet-lagged we managed to struggle out of the chaos and find them. As Ben had been living on a low budget for a year we were soon jostled towards India's cheapest mode of transport, the local bus. It looked ancient and I was convinced it would never manage the long ride into Delhi city.

Our first impressions were of sharp images of life glimpsed through the bus window. It took about an hour to reach the city along a road marked by small dwellings and shanty towns made out of paper, cardboard, rubber, tin, in fact anything that the poor could get their hands on. Even though I had witnessed such scenes as a child and heard of India's poverty, I was still bewildered at the extreme deprivation we were to come across during our stay.

TRAVEL WRITING

This is a personal account. The writer includes factual details and opinions but there are also lots of personal details such as the ones below.

- *I was really no more knowledgeable about what to expect than any other Western traveller.*

- *Even though I had witnessed such scenes as a child and heard of India's poverty …*

ACTIVITY 4

Think of a place you have visited recently. It need not have been for the first time.

Write two sentences about each of the following:

- your thoughts on the place before you got there

- how you felt when you arrived

- your feelings about the people you were with

- your thoughts on the place halfway through the visit

- how you felt when you left.

Sometimes informative writing can be very personal. You may be asked to tell your reader about something that has happened to you or to someone you know. In the following account a teenage girl informs the readers of a teenage magazine about her brother's gambling habit:

Gambling

'My brother, Kevin, is 15 and is addicted to playing fruit machines. I'm not sure when it started – we only found out about it when he was caught stealing money in town . . .

'He started hanging out in the amusement arcade in town. I knew that's where he went, because one of the boys in my class mentioned seeing him there. I asked Kevin about it at the time, and he just shrugged and said he'd nipped into the arcade to get out of the rain one day.

'He began staying out of the house a lot more. Mum and Dad didn't ask him what he got up to, until they got a letter home from school, saying that Kevin had been absent without permission. Dad was really angry, but Kevin didn't seem too bothered. He said he'd stayed off a couple of times to avoid a maths class he hated, and he promised not to do it again.

'A short while after that, money began to go missing in the house. One day I heard Dad asking Mum if she'd taken ten pounds that he'd put down. Mum said that she hadn't, but mentioned that she'd misplaced a fiver from her purse. Any pound coins or fifty pence pieces that were lying on the kitchen unit disappeared too. I suspected Kevin, though I felt guilty about thinking he was a thief. I decided to ask the boy in my class if he'd seen Kevin in the amusement arcade again and he told me he was there all the time.

'I couldn't exactly grass on my own brother, even when I realized that there was money missing from the bank in my room. I tried to speak to him, but he was pretty bad-tempered all the time.

'Although I'd worked out that Kevin was spending all his time down at the amusement arcade, Mum and Dad didn't have a clue. Because they had no idea about what Kevin was up to, they were totally shocked when the police showed up at the door. They said Kevin had been caught stealing a charity collection box from a shop counter in town . . .

'The police told them that Kevin had a serious problem with fruit machines and that he should get counselling of some sort. The shop had agreed not to press charges, as they'd got their money back, so Kevin got off with a warning. After the police left, he admitted he'd been stealing money from them both, and from me, and that he was spending about fifty pounds a week on fruit machines and had stolen from shops before.

'Mum watches Kevin all the time now. She takes him to Gamblers Anonymous, and he's been to see a counsellor. They say the only way for him to beat his addiction is to give up the machines completely. Things at home are pretty horrible – everyone is scared Kevin will get into trouble again. I feel sorry for him, though I think he was a fool to get so hooked on the machines to start with. Even though Kevin has promised never to go near the arcade again, and I think he means it, I still keep my bank hidden in my room . . .'

ACTIVITY 5

The writer has grouped her ideas together to include the various things that have happened. Arrange the following into the order in which the writer deals with them:

a Kevin's confession

b stealing from the writer

c involvement of the police

d how the habit started

e truancy

f the present situation

g stealing from the parents.

The writer uses paragraphs to organize her information. Match your list to the first sentence of each paragraph. The first one is done for you.

d how the habit started – *He started hanging out in the amusement arcade in town.*

Test *yourself*

I am a student from New Zealand. My family are moving to the United Kingdom and I will be going to school there. I know very little about the country or the people. Could your readers write to me with any information they think might help me?

Yours with thanks,

John Simmons

You read the above letter in your favourite magazine and decide to reply. Write a letter to John informing him about your home town or area and the people in it.

1 Your purpose and audience are clear – to inform John about your home area and the people in it.

2 Start to plan your letter by making a list of the different things you want to say about:

- your home area
- the people in it.

3 Your list should include both facts and opinions. Count how many facts and opinions you have written down.

4 What personal details could you include? They might be to do with where you live and how long you've lived there or particular things that have happened to you. Make a list of these.

5 Is there anything else you want to say? It might, for example, be helpful to include some details about your school and the way schools generally are run in this country.

6 You are now ready to start organizing your ideas. Remember that one of your aims is to write in *paragraphs*. Think of writing four paragraphs. Decide which ideas fit together best and the order in which you want to write them. Number them 1–4 depending on which paragraph you want to put them in.

7 Once you have organized your ideas you are ready to start writing. When writing an informal letter there are certain things you need to know. You put your address in the top right-hand corner and the date underneath this. Start your letter with the words *Dear John*, placed under the date but on the left-hand side of the page. Your letter should be written in paragraphs. End informally with *Best wishes*, *All the best*, or something similar.

8 When you have finished writing, check through your work carefully. Have you said everything you wanted to say? Are your ideas expressed clearly? Do you want to add anything or take anything out? Finally, don't forget to sign your letter!

Writing to explain

When you are *writing to explain* your aim is to tell your reader why or how something has happened, is happening or will happen. You give the *reasons* for something. The extracts on pages 95–97 show the same situation from two very different points of view. In the first extract a mother explains what happened when her daughter was late home from school. Read the extracts and the notes in the margin carefully.

The mother

I began to worry and fidget by half past five. Two buses had gone by and she had not come home from school. I thought of all the places she could go to and became afraid because there were so many. My husband was working in Glasgow and my
5 father, who stayed with us, was on holiday. The house was empty. I was afraid. Not of being alone but she would have phoned to tell me if she was going away anywhere. My stomach turned, I felt hungry but could not eat, tired but could not sleep, tormented by my imagination.
10 At six o'clock I phoned her friend but she had no idea where she was and suggested I phone several people who were other schoolfriends. I phoned them all but no one knew and said they would phone back if they found out where she was. I took the car into town. There was a girl she was friendly with
15 who lived in a house on the way to town. She hadn't a phone so I went to the door.
'Elaine, have you seen Cathie?' It was hard to speak as the cries of pain echoed through my head. I was too embarrassed to stay, I had started to cry and my eyes were red and sore. I
20 went into all the cafés she talked of. It was no use. I went home and found myself waiting for the phone to ring. It did several times. Always someone to ask if I had found her. At nine o'clock I answered the phone for the millionth time. It was Mrs Wilson, Elaine's mother. She said Cathie was at their
25 house. I felt as though the greatest load had been lifted from my heart. Again I took the car and drove into town. Cathie was very quiet and looked at me coldly. She thanked Elaine and got into the car. We said nothing but I wanted to be   ↓*cont…*

explains why she was worried

explains what she did

explains how she felt when she got the phone call from Elaine's mother

angry, I wanted to show how worried I had been. I knew that
30 she would not see my anger as love for her. It seemed as
though she hated me and wanted to hurt me, but I could tell
as she sat stiffly and unmoved that she had no idea that this
was possible. I was as pleasant as I could be and she answered
all the countless questions in a calm indifferent manner. I had
35 failed. I could not get through to her. She could not see the
agony I had gone through because of her. It was my fault she
was as she was. I had brought myself pain.

explains why she wanted to be angry and why she kept her anger in

explains why she felt she had failed

A MOTHER'S FONDNESS BY MARION RACHEL STEWART

ACTIVITY 1

Reread the extract above and try to answer these questions.

1 Why was the mother worried?

2 What did she do?

3 How did she feel when Elaine's mother rang?

4 Why did she want to be angry?

5 Why did she not show her anger?

6 Why did she feel she had failed?

Notice how the writing clearly answers these **why** and **how** questions.

In the next extract it is the daughter's turn to explain what happened:

The daughter

After school I met Caroline and as she had borrowed some records of mine I decided to go round to her house and collect them. I didn't feel like going home anyway – perhaps it was because I was getting annoyed with my mother – well, not annoyed but it had become too tense being with her.

5　We couldn't have a conversation without it becoming a row. I think she resented me a bit. I don't know why. It made things easier when I went out; I didn't have to face up to her. She really annoyed me sometimes because any row was forgotten too quickly, as though it was a routine, as though she wasn't bothered. She made me feel foolish and small. It was

10　horrible, I hated it happening. I had begun to keep out of her way as much as possible.

　　Caroline and I had a good long talk about school and other things that worried us. We listened to records for ages in complete silence, not saying a word. I suddenly realized I had missed both buses and would have to

15　try and get the eight o'clock one.

Caroline decided we should go to the loch until it was time for my bus. By the time we had walked across the causeway and back I had missed it.

　　'Mum'll go daft,' I said suddenly, beginning to worry.

　　'Look, she's going to be mad anyway so it doesn't matter how late

20　you are.'

　　'No, I'd better go now,' I said. I left and started walking through town. I was passing Elaine's house so I went in to see her.

　　'Your mother's going daft, she's been phoning everyone. She was here, she was in town twice, she's even been to the police station.' Elaine

25　stopped and took my arm.

　　'Oh God,' I said, 'Oh no, you're joking!'

　　I sat down and buried my face in my hands. She would be furious. What was I going to say to her? This meant another row.

　　'Elaine, I don't want to go home. Can't I stay here?'

30　　'You'll have to face up to her as soon as possible. That's typical of you Cathie, run away from everything. You'll have to face up to it.'

　　Mrs Wilson came in. I was scared she would be angry too.

　　'Cathie, I'm going to the phone box to phone your mother now.'

　　My mother knocked on the door and Elaine answered. She stood

35　quietly at the living room door.

　　I was angry. There had been so much fuss and now she was acting as if nothing had happened. I thanked Elaine and got into the car. I didn't see any point in talking about it so I kept very quiet and pretended I wasn't bothered. She didn't even ask where I'd been until we were halfway home.

40　　There was no way I could show her how hurt I really was. She simply didn't care about me and I couldn't let her see how much that hurts. It was no good: she had already forgotten it – just like everything else.

explains why she didn't go home straight away

explains how she came to miss the buses

explains how she felt when Elaine tells her about her mother

explains why she felt angry and hurt

A MOTHER'S FONDNESS BY
MARION RACHEL STEWART

ACTIVITY 2

Reread the daughter's side of the story and then answer these questions.

1 Why didn't Cathie go home?

2 How did she miss the buses?

3 How did she feel when she heard her Mum had been looking for her?

4 Why did she feel angry and hurt?

ACTIVITY 3

Imagine you have been called in to help the mother and daughter to solve their differences. Explain:

● the mother's point of view to the daughter

● the daughter's point of view to the mother.

Organizing an explanation

In the following extract a teenage boy explains some of the difficulties he has had at school and how he is starting to sort them out:

I don't remember having any problems at primary school. The trouble really started when I went to secondary. I was used to a small school where everybody knew everybody else – if anything went wrong my Mam always got to know and it was sorted pretty quickly. When I went to secondary it was different. Most of my friends had gone to other schools and I had
5 to start making friends quickly. Looking back, I guess the friends I made just weren't into school work and some of them enjoyed making life difficult for the teachers.

My reports in Years 7 and 8 were OK. Some of the teachers said I could do better but most of them said I was making satisfactory progress. By Year 9 it was a different story. I'd given up on work altogether and was desperate to impress my friends. Before I knew where I was I was
10 being sent out of class, put on report and given endless detentions. My report at the end of that year was a disaster. My parents went up to the school and when they got home my Dad was blazing and my Mam wouldn't even talk to me.

After that life got pretty bad. They tried to make me stay in and do my homework and I did everything I could to avoid it. Most of the time I'd get in from school, grab some tea and
15 then clear off before they got back from work. There was usually a shouting match when I got home but there wasn't really anything they could do. Sometimes, just to keep the peace, I'd go up to my room and pretend to do some work but I'd always end up listening to music.

It wasn't until Year 11 that things started to settle a bit. I knew I had big exams coming up and that I had to start doing some work for them but by that time I was way behind with my
20 assignments and didn't have a clue how to catch up. Then I met my girlfriend Cathy. She's really helped and sometimes I do my work round at her place. Things are better with Mam and Dad now as well. At least they've given up moaning at me. I know I've blown getting really good results but I'm hoping they'll be good enough to get me on the engineering course I want to do when I finish school. If I get that far I'll count myself lucky.

Chris, North London

ACTIVITY 4

Chris organizes his explanation into four paragraphs. In the first he explains why there were no problems in primary school and why he had to make friends quickly in secondary school. What does he explain in the next three paragraphs?

Test yourself

Think of something that has happened – either at school or at home – that has had a strong impact on you. Explain:

- what happened
- why and how it happened
- how you felt about it
- why it was so important.

Follow the steps outlined below.

1 Decide what you are going to write about. Here are some suggestions:

- meeting someone new
- the death of someone you cared about
- a mistake you made
- winning a competition
- witnessing an accident
- winning an important match.

2 Once you have made your choice you need to gather plenty of ideas together.

3 Use the bullet points at the top of the page to sort your ideas into a plan.

A poor plan about winning a competition would look something like this:

> - what happened: won swimming competition
> - why and how it happened: best one there — won by 5 metres
> - how you felt about it: really happy
> - why it was so important: because I'd always wanted to win it.

With a plan like this you're not going to be able to write very much.

A much better plan would look something like this:

> - what happened: won swimming competition — 6 months ago — county swimming championships — entered for 200 metres crawl — spent all morning watching other races — really nervous — friends were there — and family — all cheering me on
> - why and how it happened: a lot of training (give details) — selected for county after winning other competitions — my coach — other swimmers in the race — whistle blew — good dive — neck and neck at halfway — felt really strong — thought of all the hard work — concentrated on finishing — realised I'd won
> - how you felt about it: really happy — excited — jumped out of pool — hugged friends — proud when receiving medal — went out to celebrate
> - why it was so important: always wanted to win — worked hard — other people's efforts — sense of achievement — proved I could do it.

Using a plan like this will help you to explain clearly and in detail.

4 Once you have made your plan you are ready to start writing. Start a new paragraph for each new bullet point.

5 When you have finished writing, check through your work carefully. Have you expressed your ideas clearly? Do you want to add anything or take anything out?

Writing to describe

When *writing to describe* your aim is to make the place or the people or the thing you are describing seem real to the reader. You are trying to paint a picture with words and to make your description interesting to read.

Detail

Brian Keenan was a lecturer in a university in Beirut. On his way to work one morning in 1985 he was kidnapped. It was four and a half years before he was released. In the following extract he describes his prison cell:

I had, of course, like all of us, seen prison cells. We have all seen films about prisoners, or read books about prison life. Some of the great stories of escape and imprisonment are part of our history. It seems much of our culture is laden with these stories. But when I think back to that cell, I know
5 that nothing that I had seen before could compare with that most dismal of places. I will describe it briefly to you, that you may see it for yourself.
   It was built very shoddily of rough-cut concrete blocks haphazardly put together and joined by crude slapdash cement-work. Inside, and only on the inside, the walls were plastered over with that same dull grey cement.
10 There was no paint. There was no colour, just the constant monotony of rough grey concrete. The cell was six feet long and four feet wide. I could stand up and touch those walls with my outstretched hands and walk those six feet in no more than four paces. On the floor was a foam mattress. With the mattress laid out I had a pacing stage of little more
15 than a foot's width.
   In one corner there was a bottle of water which I replenished daily when I went to the toilet, and in another corner was a bottle for urine, which I took with me to empty. There was also a plastic cup in which I kept a much abused and broken toothbrush. On the mattress was an old, ragged,
20 filthy cover. It had originally been a curtain. There was one blanket which I never used, due to the heat, the filth and the heavy smell, stale and almost putrid, of the last person who had slept here. The cell had no windows. A sheet steel door was padlocked every day, sounding like a thump on the head to remind me where I was. At the head of the mattress
25 I kept my briefcase with my school text books. Behind the briefcase I hid my shoes. I was forever afraid that I would lose those shoes. If I did, I felt it would be a sure sign that I would never leave that cell.

AN EVIL CRADLING BY BRIAN KEENAN

One of the secrets of a good description is to give your reader plenty of detail. Here is an artist's impression of Brian Keenan's cell. How closely does it match the description given in the second paragraph?

ACTIVITY 1

Reread the third paragraph. List the details you would now change or add to the picture.

Adjectives

It is not just the detail that is important in the extract on page 100. The words that are chosen to describe things help the reader to build up an accurate picture. Look at the following:

- <u>crude slapdash</u> cement-work
- <u>rough grey</u> concrete
- a <u>much abused</u> and <u>broken</u> toothbrush
- an <u>old</u>, <u>ragged</u>, <u>filthy</u> cover
- the <u>heavy</u> smell, <u>stale</u> and <u>almost putrid</u>.

The words that are underlined are being used to tell you more about the cement-work, the concrete, the toothbrush, the cover and the smell. When used in this way, these words are called *adjectives*.

ACTIVITY 2

Try to think of words that could be used to describe:

- a new toothbrush
- a pleasant smell.

How many suitable words can you think of?

Organization

A good description also contains well-organized ideas. Notice how, in Brian Keenan's description, one idea often leads on to another:

> At the head of the mattress I kept my briefcase with my school text books. Behind the briefcase I hid my shoes. I was forever afraid that I would lose those shoes. If I did, I felt it would be a sure sign that I would never leave that cell.

Keenan links the briefcase to the shoes, his fear of losing the shoes and the reason for this fear. The ideas follow on from each other even though they are separated by the sentence organization.

ACTIVITY 3

Copy out and complete the following sentences. Then write two more sentences which continue the same ideas:

At the foot of my bed I kept my school bag with my books. Behind the bag I hid my _____ .

Brian Keenan's room was a prison cell. There were very few things in it. In the following extract John Steinbeck describes a room that is full of things:

Crooks, the negro stable buck, had his bunk in the harness room; a little shed that leaned off the wall of the barn. On one side of the little room there was a square four-paned window, and on the other a narrow plank door leading
5 into the barn. Crooks' bunk was a long box filled with straw, on which his blankets were flung. On the wall by the window there were pegs on which hung broken harness in process of being mended, strips of new leather; and under the window itself a little bench for leather-
10 working tools, curved knives and needles and ball of linen thread, and a small hand-riveter. On pegs were also pieces of harness, a split collar with the horsehair stuffing out, a broken hame, and a trace chain with its leather covering split. Crooks had his apple-box over his bunk, and in it a
15 range of medicine bottles, both for himself and for the horses. There were cans of saddle soap and a drippy can of tar with its paint-brush sticking over the edge. And scattered about the floor were a number of personal possessions; for, being alone, Crooks could leave his things
20 about, and being a stable buck and a cripple, he was more permanent than the other men, and he had accumulated more possessions than he could carry on his back. ↓*cont...*

Crooks possessed several pairs of shoes, a pair of rubber boots, a big alarm clock and a single-barrelled shotgun.
25 And he had books, too: a tattered dictionary and a mauled copy of the California civil code for 1905. There were battered magazines and a few dirty books on a special shelf over his bunk. A pair of large gold-rimmed spectacles hung from a nail on the wall above his bed.

OF MICE AND MEN BY JOHN STEINBECK

Like Keenan, Steinbeck also uses *adjectives* to help describe things.

ACTIVITY 4

Descriptions often come alive if you use lots of adjectives. Write down the adjectives that are used to describe:

- the window (line 4)
- the possessions (lines 23–4)
- the dictionary (line 25)
- the harness (line 8)
- the thread (line 11)
- the magazines (line 27)
- the can of tar (lines 16–17)
- the spectacles (line 28).

Steinbeck tells us some things about Crooks directly. We learn that he was a negro, a stable buck, that he was alone, that he was a cripple and that he had more possessions than he could carry. The detailed description of his room, however, tells us many more things about him.

ACTIVITY 5

Look at the description of Crooks's bed in lines 5–6. What does this tell you?

What do you learn about the type of work Crooks does from the details in lines 6–17?

Make a list of his personal possessions as described in the second paragraph. What does each of these belongings tell you about him?

ACTIVITY 6

Think about an elderly woman who rarely sees her family. What possessions do you think you might find in her room? Make a list of them. Decide what each possession tells you about her.

Atmosphere and mood

Descriptions often do more than tell you about a place or a person.
They create a sense of atmosphere or mood. In the following extract
Maya Angelou describes the Store owned by her grandmother:

> Until I was thirteen and left Arkansas for good, the Store was my favorite place to be.
> Alone and empty in the mornings, it looked like an unopened present from a stranger.
> Opening the front doors was pulling the ribbon off the unexpected gift. The light
> would come in softly (we faced north), easing itself over shelves of mackerel, salmon,
> tobacco, thread. It fell flat on the big vat of lard and by noontime during the summer
> the grease had softened to a thick soup. Whenever I walked into the Store in the
> afternoon, I sensed that it was tired. I alone could hear the slow pulse of its job half
> done. But just before bedtime, after numerous people had walked in and out, had
> argued over their bills or joked about their neighbors, or just dropped in 'to give
> Sister Henderson a "Hi y'all",' the promise of magic mornings returned to the Store
> and spread itself over the family in washed life waves.

I KNOW WHY THE CAGED BIRD SINGS BY MAYA ANGELOU

ACTIVITY 7

Copy out the following passage, filling in the missing quotations:

Maya Angelou describes the Store as though it were like a person, saying it is
'Alone _____ mornings'. She compares it to an 'unopened _____ from
a _____'. She carries on this comparison by saying that 'Opening the front
doors was pulling _____ gift'. This gets across the sense of excitement and
wonder she felt every morning when she walked into the Store. She creates a sense of
peace and calm by saying that the light came in 'softly _____ over' the shelves
in the Store. In the afternoon she senses that the Store 'was _____ '. The Store
is like a person to her and in the afternoon it has a 'slow _____ done'.
Later 'the promise of _____ in washed life waves'. This suggests that the Store
was a special place that gave life and energy to the family.

By giving the Store human characteristics Maya Angelou helps the reader not
only to see it but also to feel it and to get a sense of what it was like to be in it.
She creates a mood or atmosphere by describing the place in this way.

ACTIVITY 8

Think of what a football stadium is like when it is:

- full
- empty.

Make a list of words that describe it at these different times.

Make a list of things you could compare it to in order to capture its mood or atmosphere.

Test *yourself*

Describe a room you know well. It could be your bedroom, a classroom or somewhere else. Aim to make your description interesting for your reader.

1 Picture the room in your mind. Make a list of details about:

- the size and shape of the room
- the colours in the room
- the furniture in the room.

For each item in your list think of **adjectives** that help to describe it more clearly, e.g. an *almost perfect* square, a *jet black* carpet, an *old* and *worn* desk.

2 Think about the person or people who spend time in the room. What personal possessions, such as books, magazines, posters and photographs, are in the room? Remember some of these will be hidden from sight in cupboards and under the bed. Make a list of the possessions. For each item think of adjectives that describe it more clearly, e.g. the *battered* but *much loved* bear, the *faded, life-size* Oasis poster.

3 Think about what the room feels like. Does it feel differently at different times of the day? Which of these words best suit the way it feels?

- cheerful
- comforting
- dismal
- light
- interesting
- eerie
- depressing
- bright
- dark
- private
- boring
- frightening.

4 Decide where you are going to be. Are you going to be in the room describing what you see from the inside? Or are you going to be looking in at it from the outside?

5 Decide on the order in which you are going to write. Here is one possible way of sequencing your ideas:

paragraph 1: the size, shape and colours of the room – the feel of it when you first walk into it or look at it

paragraph 2: the furniture in the room and where it's placed

paragraph 3: the personal possessions that can be seen

paragraph 4: the personal possessions that are hidden away

paragraph 5: what the room tells you about the person who owns it.

6 Think of a good way of starting your description. Here are some suggestions for an opening sentence.

a I rubbed the dirty window pane and peered through it to see a small and very untidy bedroom.

b Lying on my bed I looked around my room and sighed.

c I opened the door into the empty room and looked around it slowly.

7 Decide on your opening sentence and write your description.

8 When you have finished, read through your description carefully. Does it paint a picture of the room in your mind? Are there any details or words you could add to make the picture clearer?

Section C
EXAM PRACTICE

PAPER 1

*This paper examines **Reading** in Section A and **Writing** in Section B. Each section is worth 15% of your final mark for English.*

Section A asks you to write about non-fiction materials. These may include extracts from autobiographies, biographies, journals, diaries, letters, travel writing, leaflets, newspaper articles, factual and informative materials. You will be asked to show that you:

- understand what the materials are about
- can tell the difference between fact and opinion
- can follow an argument
- are aware of how the materials are presented
- can select the right information to answer the questions.

Section B requires one piece of writing which instructs, persuades or argues, linked to the theme(s) or topic(s) of the stimulus materials in Section A. You will be asked to show that you can:

- present your work neatly and clearly
- spell and punctuate correctly
- organize your ideas into sentences and paragraphs
- communicate your ideas clearly
- use a range of appropriate words
- show awareness of audience and purpose.

Exam Practice – Foundation Tier

PAPER 1

Time: 2 hours

Instructions to candidates

- Answer *Question 1* from Section A and *one* question from Section B.
- Spend about one hour on Section A and about one hour on Section B.
- You must *not* use a dictionary in this exam.

SECTION A

- Answer all parts of the question that follow.
- Spend *about one hour* on this section.

1   **a)**   Read Text A

      i According to the article, what advantages can children gain from working?

      ii What points does the writer make to support the view that children must be protected from the dangers of work?

    b)   Read Text B

      i What are the differences in the rules for working on Saturdays for children who are 13 and those who are 15?

    Read Text C

      ii Explain why some head teachers want to limit the working hours of their pupils.

    c)   All *three* texts are connected with young people and work. Compare *two* of these, explaining which you think is the most informative and why.

        You should comment on:

      i what they are about

      ii the ways the information is presented

      iii the ways the writers use language.

DANGER!
children at work

Work is not a dirty word. Not always. Sometimes work done by children and young people brings benefits all round.

It can provide vital income for families. It can lead young people towards independence, giving a sense of achievement and self-worth. It can help young people learn.

BUT . . . sometimes it damages health, stunts development and ruins young lives. Sometimes it kills.

From slavery to assassination

When he was four, Iqbal Masih was sold to a carpet factory owner. He spent the next six years tying knots on a carpet loom. He started work at 4 a.m., and for the twelve hour shift was chained to the loom.

Local activists freed him when he was ten. Then he travelled widely, speaking out against the evils of the bonded carpet trade. He spoke at an international conference in Stockholm last year about the terrible conditions of the 6 million child workers in Pakistan. As well as praise for his work, he also received death threats, believed to be from the powerful carpet mafia.

In December Iqbal received a Youth in Action award. He set aside the £10,000 prize for his education. He planned to become a lawyer, and had been offered a scholarship at a Boston University.

One Sunday last April Iqbal Masih was shot dead as he rode his bicycle around his village in Pakistan. He was twelve years old.

Illegal exploitation . . .

Don't get the idea that children work in dangerous jobs only in poor countries. Earlier this year a firm in Staffordshire was fined for employing children illegally at a paper and packaging factory.

One boy had worked there since he was thirteen. Along with other children he worked weekday shifts of up to six hours starting at 4 p.m. At weekends they worked shifts longer than eight hours.

Inspectors found dangerous equipment and fittings that could have caused amputation and electrocution.

The company director said at the trial that she knew of a great number of similar businesses with the same working conditions.

Death by misadventure – in a factory

A 15-year-old Birmingham school student died this year after breathing solvent fumes and collapsing into a vat of water.

He was working to save money for his favourite sport of angling. It is illegal to employ anyone under school-leaving age in a factory.

We're NOT talking about paper rounds

No one has ever seriously threatened paper rounds or casual work like baby-sitting. What we do want, however, is to protect young people from exploitation. That means:
● dangerous jobs in unsafe conditions
● hours of work that interfere with school, or are so long they might damage health.

Last century Britain was well known for exploiting children. They worked in coal mines, in factories, on farms and (as everyone knows) up chimneys.

Such work was dirty and dangerous and appalling. It was ended by protection laws.

Today **we** must make sure **our** children are protected from the dangers of work.

SOURCED FROM *ESSENTIAL ARTICLES IV*, THE RESOURCE FILE FOR ISSUES, CAREL PRESS

B ▼

GUIDE TO HOURS OF EMPLOYMENT FOR CHILDREN OF COMPULSORY SCHOOL AGE

1. No child shall be employed until he or she has reached the age of thirteen years.

2. A child who has reached the age of thirteen years may be employed before school between 7.00 a.m. and 8.00 a.m. in the delivery of milk or newspapers, but if so employed, shall not be employed after school hours in any occupation for a period of more than one hour between the hours of 4.30 p.m. and 6.30 p.m. If a child works both mornings and evenings it must be for the same employer.

3. No child under the age of fifteen years shall be employed on any Saturday or other school holiday for more than five hours or before 7.00 a.m. or after 7.00 p.m, or for more than 25 hours in any week.

4. No child who has reached the age of fifteen years shall be employed for more than eight hours on any Saturday or other school holiday, or before 7.00 a.m. or after 7.00 p.m., or for more than 35 hours in any week.

5. No child shall be employed on Sundays except in the delivery of milk or newspapers for more than one hour, and that hour shall only be between the hours of 8.00 a.m. and 10.00 a.m.

PROHIBITED EMPLOYMENT
YOU WILL <u>NOT</u> BE GRANTED A PERMIT FOR THE FOLLOWING OCCUPATIONS:-

1. In a Hairdressers with contact wth harmful chemicals.

2. Working in the kitchens of a Hotel/Cafe or similar establishment.

3. Using machinery in Shops.

4. Working in Pubs, Clubs etc i.e. glass collecting, or in an Off-Licence.

5. Selling programmes/refreshments etc in a registered or licensed club or a place of public entertainment.

6. Collecting unwanted refuse.

7. Working in fair grounds or amusement arcades.

8. Working in a Slaughter house.

9. Working in, or in connection with, any Racecourse or Track or other place where any sport is carried on.

10. Working in Mobile shops and Discotheques.

11. Agricultural work or any work involving heavy strain.

12. In connection with football pools, betting shops, or a lottery.

13. The delivery of fuel oils.

14. <u>Outside</u> window cleaning more than 10 feet above ground level.

MIDDLESBROUGH BOROUGH EDUCATION AUTHORITY LEAFLET

Work in shops till the grades drop

'We believe students studying full-time can cope with a maximum of eight hours' paid work each week. Unfortunately, our students are experiencing enormous pressure from the managers of stores to work up to 30 hours each week,' said Margaret Edwards, head of Wallington High School, Sutton.

The school estimates that 87% of its sixth-formers are working, with at least one in five doing more than 10 hours a week.

Chris Tarrant, head of Wilson's, a boys' school also in Wallington, believes more students are working longer – and often for social as much as for financial reasons.

'One wants to encourage the pupils to work. It is good to manage your own finances and it gives you a bit more freedom if you can run your own car,' he said. 'But it is an issue that is ultimately going to affect our results. The thing is to know the boys are going to be fulfilling their potential at this stage of their lives.'

Union research suggests that under-18s are working long hours even for reputable firms. 'Employers using school kids are saving themselves £400 million a year by employing children rather than adults,' according to Rory Faulkener, chairperson of the GMB union's young members advisory committee.

Sixteen and 17-year-olds had traditionally been paid less than older staff. 'Students could be putting their long-term educational prospects in danger for the sake of a quick buck,' he said.

Shops are putting pressure on sixth-formers to work long hours – which is affecting their A-level performance, it has been claimed.

The heads of two Surrey schools are so concerned about the performance of their 'exhausted' sixth-formers they are sending out letters to employers who ask for references.

The letters say they do not want students accepting employment during the school day or taking on more than eight hours' work a week.

SECTION B

Answer *one* question in this section.

- You can use some of the information from Section A if you want to, but you do not have to do so.
- Spend *about one hour* on this section.

Remember:

- spend ten minutes planning and sequencing your material
- try to write at least two sides
- spend ten minutes checking:
    your paragraphing
    your punctuation
    your spelling.

Either

1   Should young people be allowed to work?

Write an article for a teenage magazine in which you **argue** either for or against young people being allowed to work while still at school.

Or

2   Write a letter to an employer of your choice in which you try to **persuade** him or her to take you on for a three-month trial period. You should include details on:

- what it is you hope to do
- why you want this job
- your skills and experience
- the personal qualities you will bring to the job.

Or

3   Write an advice sheet for young people who are considering taking on part-time work. **Instruct** them on:

- the advantages and disadvantages of part-time work
- ways to go about getting a job
- how to cope with school work and part-time work.

The examiner comments . . .

SECTION A

1 a) i The possible advantages of children working are given to you at the start of the article. One is that it can provide vital income for families. What are the others?

ii This question is asking you to follow the argument by picking out the key points. The first thing the writer does is show you how cruelly some children are treated at work. He does this by telling you about Iqbal Masih who worked for twelve hours a day from the age of four, during which time he was chained to the loom. The next point he makes is that it is not just children in poor countries who work long hours and in dangerous conditions. An example is given of children working for a firm in Staffordshire.

What other key points can you select?

b) i Here you are being asked to pick out different bits of information and compare them. You will find the relevant information under numbers 3 and 4 in the first list. Point 3 tells you that a child under fifteen cannot work for more than five hours on a Saturday and not before 7 a.m. or after 7 p.m. What are the differences and similarities between this and the information given to you in point 4?

ii To answer this question you need to look closely at the opinions expressed by the heads in this article. One reason is that they are concerned about the performance of their exhausted sixth formers. Can you find two others?

c) You are asked to compare two of the three texts. Whichever you pick, your answer must include comments on the things listed in the bullet points. Say what both texts are about and point out any similarities or differences between them. When writing about the ways the information is presented you could comment on headlines, sub-headings, the way the information is organized, different types of print and the use of photographs. When looking at language think about the different kinds of writing from the straightforward instructions in Text B to the emotive 'sometimes it damages health, stunts development and ruins young lives' in Text A. Pick out and comment on particular words and phrases. There's plenty that could be said just about the two headlines, '**Danger! children at work**' and '**Work in shops till the grades drop**'.

SECTION B

Whichever task you choose there are certain things you need to remember. Make sure you:

- know who you are writing for
- know why you are writing
- know what you are writing
- know the kind of writing you are being asked to do.

For example:

Should young people be allowed to work?

Write an article for a teenage magazine in which you argue either for or against young people being allowed to work while still at school.

Notes

- *audience: teenage readers*
- *purpose: to argue for or against young people being allowed to work*
- *what you are writing: an article*
- *kind of writing: writing to argue.*

Once you have broken down the task in this way remember to:

- gather ideas together
- sequence your ideas
- think about the kind of language you should use
- think about the way you should set your writing out.

Once you have completed your writing:

- read through carefully to check it makes clear sense
- add or delete words for greater effect
- correct any mistakes in spelling and punctuation.

PAPER 2

*This paper examines **Reading** in Section A and **Writing** in Section B. Each section is worth 15% of your final mark for English.*

Section A asks you to write about prepared poetry. The poetry appears as part of the **NEAB Anthology**, consisting of a selection from the work of *three* poets in the English literary tradition together with a selection of poems from other cultures and traditions. You will be asked to show that you can:

- understand what the poems are about
- select the right information to answer the questions
- write about the ways the poets present their ideas through form and language
- make appropriate reference to the poems.

Section B requires *one* piece of writing which informs, explains or describes. Some of these tasks may be linked to themes in the **Anthology** poems studied for Section A. You will be asked to show that you can:

- present your work neatly and clearly
- spell and punctuate correctly
- organize your ideas into sentences and paragraphs
- communicate your ideas clearly
- use a range of appropriate words
- show awareness of audience and purpose.

Exam Practice – Foundation Tier

PAPER 2

Time: 2 hours

Instructions to candidates

- Answer *three* questions. Answer *one* question from Section A Part 1 (*Poets*), *one* question from Section A Part 2 (*Poems from Other Cultures and Traditions*) and *one* question from Section B.
- You should spend about *one hour* on Section A and *one hour* on Section B.
- You must *not* use a dictionary in this exam.

SECTION A PART 1: Poets

Base your answers on the work of the poet you have studied in your **Anthology**.

Either

1   Write about the way the poet makes situations *or* places real for the reader. You should comment on:

- the ways the ideas are organized
- the words the poet uses.

Refer to at least *two* poems in your answer.

Or

2   Choose *two* poems which have had a strong effect on you. Write about:

- what the poems are about
- the way you feel about the poems.
- the ways words are used

SECTION A PART 2: Poems from Other Cultures and Traditions

Base your answers on the Poems from Other Cultures and Traditions in your **Anthology.**

Either

3   Choose *two* poems which tell you something about the beliefs and customs of a different culture. Explain:

- what you have learnt
- how the poet has got the ideas across to you.

Or

4   Choose *two* poems in which you find the poets' use of language interesting. Explain your choice by writing about the ways the poets use language.

SECTION B

- Answer *one* question from this section.
- You should spend *about one hour* on this section.

Remember:

- spend ten minutes planning and sequencing your material
- try to write at least two sides
- spend ten minutes checking:
    your paragraphing
    your punctuation
    your spelling.

Either

1   Many people have interests to which they give a great deal of time, effort and sometimes money. Write **informatively** about an interest of yours, making clear what it is, what it involves and why it is important to you.

Or

2   Money doesn't always bring happiness.

   Explain what you would do if you suddenly won a lot of money and the reasons for the choices you would make.

Or

3   **Describe** a person you know well. Aim to make your description lively and interesting.

The examiner comments . . .

SECTION A PARTS 1 AND 2

Working with your Anthology

When you start to study the poems in your **Anthology** you need to think about:

- meaning
- presentation
- language.

Thinking about meaning

- Ask yourself questions about the meaning of the poem: Who? What? Where? When? Why? How?
- Are there other meanings buried beneath the surface?
- Is there a particular viewpoint developed in the poem?
- Does the poem tell you something about another culture?

Thinking about presentation

- What can you say about the way the words are set out on the page?
- Is there any repetition of ideas or words? What is the effect of this?
- Is rhyme used? Where? How does it affect the way the poem is read aloud?
- Is the rhythm regular or irregular?

Thinking about language

- How does the poet use words to get across particular ideas or images?
- Are there any examples of simile, metaphor or personification? What is their effect?
- Is there anything unusual about the way the poet uses words, e.g. dialect? What is the effect of this?

Once you have thought carefully about the poems, read them again a few times and understood them, you are ready to start to develop your own point of view. The following questions are useful starting points.

- Which poems do you like most? Why?
- Which poems do you like least? Why?
- Which poems have made you see things differently? Why?
- Which poem would you most like to have written yourself? Why?

When you come to write about the poems in an examination you need to make sure that you read the questions carefully and choose the right bits of information to answer them. It is often helpful to break down a question before starting to answer it. Read the following question again.

Write about the way the poet makes situations or **places real for the reader.**

You should comment on:

- the ways the ideas are organized
- the words the poet uses.

Refer to at least *two* poems in your answer.

In order to answer this question properly you need to:

- choose two poems that are about situations or places
- write about the way the ideas are organized in each of the poems
- pick out and write about examples of words that the poet uses to make the situation or place seem real.

It is *very important* that you choose your poems carefully, work out what the question is asking you and then make sure you answer it properly.

SECTION B

This section is testing you on your ability to *inform*, *explain* or *describe*. You need to think about the different kinds of writing each question is asking for before you decide which question to answer.

Question 1 asks you to write informatively, Question 2 asks you to explain and Question 3 asks you to describe.

Before you make your choice be sure that you have plenty to write about. You have an hour to answer *one* of the three questions and are expected to write about two sides, so you will need plenty of different ideas.

Once you have made your choice remember to spend *ten minutes* gathering and sequencing your ideas. This is a very important part of the writing process and will help you to produce a much better piece of work.

As you are writing make sure that your handwriting is clear, that each sentence is carefully thought through and that your ideas are organized into paragraphs. Choose your words carefully and aim to make your writing as interesting as possible for the reader.

When you check through your work, read each word that you have written. Be on the look-out for mistakes in spelling and punctuation and correct them. If you see ways of improving your work don't be afraid to cross out words and put better ones in.

Sample Paper 1 – Foundation Tier

Time: 2 hours

Instructions to candidates

- Answer *Question 1* from Section A and *one* question from Section B.
- Spend about one hour on Section A and one hour on Section B.
- You must *not* use a dictionary in this exam.

SECTION A

- Answer all parts of the question that follows.
- Spend *about one hour* on this section.

1   a)   Read Text A

According to the article why do some children:

- become victims of bullies
- become bullies?

b)   Read Text B

i   In what different ways was Caroline bullied?
ii   How did the bullying affect her life?

c)   Both texts are about bullying. Which do you think is the most interesting and effective? You should consider:

- what they are about
- the ways they are written
- the ways they are presented.

A

Bullying:
is <u>your</u> child a victim?

Two in five school children are regularly being bullied. Anne Montague finds out who the bullies are – and how to stop their reign of terror.

The most recent study of 1,000 children aged between eight and 16, by Dr Peter Smith at the University of Sheffield, found that 20 per cent of them were bullied occasionally. Ten per cent of the children questioned had been bullied within the last week.

When Michele Elliott of Kidscape – an organization founded to keep children safe from a variety of dangers including bullying – interviewed 4,000 children she found that 38 per cent had been bullied badly enough to describe the experience as 'terrifying'. This situation can't be allowed to continue.

Why don't children tell?

It is perhaps because of the secrecy surrounding bullying that parents are the last to know. Bullying flourishes because the victim is not only vulnerable but bound by a code of 'honour' – 'it's wrong to tell tales'– and fear – 'don't tell or I'll hit you'. Other children won't tell, probably because they're afraid that they too will be bullied. We must try to break this code of silence. *cont...*

Is your child at risk?

Bullying cuts across all ages and types of school – primary as well as secondary. Victims tend to be smaller, physically weaker, not good at games, poorly co-ordinated, shy and lacking confidence. They may look different – be fat, skinny, have bad skin or a big nose or ears – or be different – very rich or very poor. Handicapped children and those with special needs suffer greatly from bullying. So do children from ethnic minorities.

Who are the bullies?

Research shows that bullies may have problems at home. They tend to come from families where physical superiority is encouraged, aggression is accepted and power is the language that gets results. In some ways bullies are also victims, unloved or subjected to violence at home.

Bullying takes many different forms, although it nearly always happens in front of other children. Punching, kicking and gang attacks are commonplace. Bullies frequently lie in wait to 'ambush' their victim. Victims often have their clothes ripped, school books torn up, and their possessions stolen. They may be forced to hand over dinner money and bus fares to the leading bully under threat of violence. It's not uncommon for victims to be spat or urinated on.

'Our interviews with children show that bullies don't understand other people's feelings or understand they're hurting other children,' says Valerie Besag, who's an educational psychologist.

WHAT TO DO IF . . .
YOU THINK YOUR CHILD IS BEING BULLIED

● Ask your child about it. If he won't tell you ask other children and parents if they know anything about it.
● Talk it over with your child, show that you take it seriously and let him know that he has your support.
● Give him practical advice. Encourage him to stay with groups and to avoid places where bullying happens.
● Go and see the school and make sure you get their help.
● Help your child find ways of dealing with this. Help him ignore the bullying and name calling, laugh at it and walk away.
● Encourage your child to take up new interests to take his mind off the bullying. Don't push him into anything he's not ready for.

. . . YOU THINK YOUR CHILD MIGHT BE A BULLY

● Talk to him in a calm way. He may well not understand the effect his behaviour is having on other children.
● Encourage him to take up other activities such as sport. This may help to direct his energies more positively.
● Bullying may be a cry for help. Has anything happened at home recently to upset him – a new baby, a divorce? If so, your child may feel unloved and insecure.
● Is there anything in your behaviour or the values at home which might encourage bullying behaviour? If so, you need to deal with it.
● If bullying persists, go to the school for help.

What are the consequences?

It's believed bullying lays the foundations for serious problems in later life – for both bullies and victims. Research from the USA shows that victims enter adult life vulnerable, socially insecure and more prone to social problems than their counterparts, while the bullies are more likely to become involved in criminal and delinquent activities.

B

'Why Do You Bully Me?'

To the people who've been bullying me

I don't know why I'm writing this, because I'll probably never have the guts to send it. If I do and you read it, you'll probably laugh at it and say I'm a wimp.

I can't understand why anyone would be a bully and it's even harder to understand why you bully me.

I wonder if any of you have ever stopped to think how I feel about it all. Probably not, or you wouldn't go along with it. None of you can have any idea how scary it is. You don't know what it's like to dread going to school every day because you know they won't leave you alone, or to stay off just to avoid them. You've no idea what it's like to cry in bed every night because you're so scared of what will happen the next day.

I've tried to stop you from bullying me, I really have. At first I just sort of put up with it and hoped you'd get fed up and leave me alone. But it just got worse – you all seemed to get angry at me for being such a loser. So then I tried to fight back, telling you to get lost. But that just made one of you mad and you started pushing me around and telling me not to make you angry or I'd regret it.

I've never been the most popular person in school but being bullied has really affected my friendships. I've still got one or two mates, but I know other people are scared to talk to me or be friends because they're worried if you see me with them, they'll end up being bullied as well.

I'll never forget the first time you singled me out. It was after an English lesson, when the teacher had read out an essay I'd written. I was walking home from school with my mate, Lisa, and I saw you behind us, but you never said anything. But as soon as Lisa left me to go down her street and I was on my own, you started shouting at me, saying I was a swot and thought I was great.

I just ignored you, but that just made you mad. You all surrounded me and started pushing me about, laughing at me. I was honestly terrified – my heart was pounding. Eventually you all ran off, thinking it had been great fun.

I hoped it would be a one-off, but every single day you'd shout at me or push me around. I suppose I could have put up with that but then you started going a bit further. A few days after you first picked on me, you even started taking my dinner money. My mates tried to persuade me to tell someone what was going on, but I didn't.

One of the worst experiences was the other day, when it was raining. I was walking home from Lisa's house and you spotted me – had you been waiting for me? When you surrounded me and started chucking stones at me, it was so scary because there were more of you. It must have been about nine against one.

When you thought someone was coming, you all ran off. I just sat there sobbing. I just couldn't see an end to it and even thought about running away from home. Then how would you have felt – would you have cared?

People always say that bullies are cowards and it's true. If I see one of you on your own, you'll mostly just ignore me or give me a dirty look. One of you sometimes even gives me a little sort of half-smile, as if to say you're sorry about what's going on. But as soon as you're with just one other member of your gang, you start picking on me again. You're pathetic, really.

It's been going on for months now and looking back, I can see I've become almost like a different person. My schoolwork's really suffered and the teachers keep saying I'll have to make more of an effort. I hardly ever laugh any more, either. Mum keeps asking me what's wrong, but I've never told her.

I've even been stealing money from Mum's purse to give to you. I've never felt so bad about anything in my life, especially when Mum said to me that her money seemed to be disappearing and she suspected a girl at her work.

You warned me from the start not to tell anyone about what was going on and I didn't. But now I'm just letting you know that I've realized keeping quiet was the biggest mistake I made.

Hitting and punching, I made myself put up with it. But what happened before the Christmas holidays made me decide that I had to speak out. I can't believe anyone would be as cruel as you were then. Pinning me down was scary enough – I just couldn't move. But then when you got out the scissors, I was so terrified. You all thought it was a great laugh to cut chunks out of my long hair, didn't you?

Afterwards, when you ran off, I picked up the hair that you'd cut off and cried. Do you really want to ruin my life? Telling Mum I'd been mucking about with a mate sounded pathetic, even to me. But what else could I say?

Now I've realized this is something I can't cope with on my own any more, which is why I've told my mum. When I made up my mind, it was such a relief. In fact, I wonder how I could have been so stupid to keep it quiet all this time. I felt so nervous telling her, but at the same time it was great to talk about it. Mum was great. She's given me brilliant advice and is coming to school to have a meeting with the headteacher about it.

I feel glad that it's going to be sorted out once and for all, although I'm scared of how you'll react. But I just tell myself it can't be any worse than what I've been going through recently with you.

I just wish this whole thing had never started. I can't believe you picked on me for an English essay. It seems so ridiculous. I never really did find out your real reason for doing it. But I think you probably don't even have a proper reason – you're just a bunch of bitches.

I don't know what sort of punishment you'll get. I don't really care, though. As long as you leave me alone and I get my life back to myself, that's all I'm bothered about. But it'll take a lot of time before I can get over what you've done to me . . .

Caroline

SECTION B

- Answer *one* question in this section.

You can use some information from Section A if you want to, but you do not have to do so.

- Spend *about one hour* on this section.

> **Remember:**
> - spend ten minutes planning and sequencing your material
> - try to write at least two sides
> - spend ten minutes checking:
>   your paragraphing
>   your punctuation
>   your spelling.

Either

1   Write an advice sheet for teachers on how they should deal with bullying in schools. Include clear **instructions** on what they should do if they think a child is being bullied.

Or

2   Should bullies be expelled from school?

    Write an article for a school magazine or newsletter **arguing** that bullying should not be tolerated in schools.

Or

3   Write a letter to parents of primary school children, aiming to **persuade** them that bullying is a serious problem, both in and out of school, and that they should be on their guard against it.

Sample Paper 2 – Foundation Tier

Time: 2 hours

Instructions to candidates

- Answer *three* questions. Answer *one* question from Section A Part 1 (*Poets*), *one* question from Section A Part 2 (*Poems from Other Cultures and Traditions*) and *one* question from Section B.
- You should spend about *one hour* on Section A and *one hour* on Section B.
- You must *not* use a dictionary in this exam.

SECTION A PART 1: Poets

Base your answers on the work of the poet you have studied in your **Anthology**.

Either

1   Choose *two* poems which tell you something about feelings. Explain:

- what the feelings are
- how the poet has described them.

Or

2   Poems are often about people. Write about the people in *two* of the poems you have studied. You should write about:

- what the people are like
- the way the poet presents them.

SECTION A PART 2: Poems from Other Cultures and Traditions

Base your answers on the *Poems from Other Cultures and Traditions* in your **Anthology**.

Either

3   Choose *two* poems where the poets present their ideas in an unusual way. Explain your choice by writing about:

- form
- language
- other features which you consider to be unusual.

Or

4   Place is an important feature of several of these poems. Write about *two* poems in which you think it is particularly important and explain why.

SECTION B

- Answer *one* question from this section.
- You should spend *about one hour* on this section.

> **Remember:**
>
> - spend ten minutes planning and sequencing your material
> - try to write at least two sides
> - spend ten minutes checking:
>   your paragraphing
>   your punctuation
>   your spelling.

Either

1   Write about a recent holiday you have had, **informing** your reader of both the good and the bad things about it.

Or

2   What would you like to be doing in five years' time? Write about your hopes for the future and **explain** how you intend to make them come true.

Or

3   Write **descriptively** about: The Place Where I Live.